Hey World! Why do I Feel All Alone in a Planet Full of People?

Learn How Technology has Made us More Lonely and How Technology Can Bring Us Together as Human Beings

Oreste J. DAversa, CPC

Life Coach

PUBLISHER'S NOTE

This book is designed to provide accurate and authoritative information. information in regard to the subject matter covered. It is sold with the understanding that neither the author nor publisher is engaged in rendering psychological, legal, or other professional service. If psychological, legal, professional advice or other expert assistance is required, the services of a professional in that field should be sought. The principles and concepts presented in this book are the opinions of the author and are based on his interpretations of the aforementioned principles. Neither the author nor publisher is liable or responsible to any person or entity for any errors contained on this book, or website, or for any special, incidental, or consequential damage caused or alleged to be caused directly or indirectly by the information contained on this book or website. Any application of the techniques, ideas, and suggestions in this book is at the reader's sole discretion and risk.

No part of this publication may be reproduced, redistributed, taught, stored in a retrieval system, or transmitted, in any form, or by any means, electronic, mechanical, photocopy, recording, or otherwise, without the prior written permission of the publisher.

Disclosure Statement: This book contains both AI-assisted and AI-generated content. The AI-assisted content was developed using tools to aid in brainstorming, editing, and refining the text, while the AI-generated content includes sections of the book created entirely by artificial intelligence. All AI-generated content has been reviewed and edited to ensure it meets the high standards of quality and originality.

FIRST EDITION

ISBN: 978-1-952294-35-8

Library of Congress Control Number: 2024915040

Published by: Cutting Edge Technology Publishing

Copyright © Oreste J. D'Aversa, 2024. All rights reserved.

TABLE OF CONTENTS

About the Author — 5

Preface — 9

Introduction: The Paradox of Connection and Isolation in the Digital Age — 11

Part I: Understanding Our Loneliness

Chapter 01: The Evolution of Communication: From Face-to-Face to Digital Interfaces — 17

Chapter 02: The Illusion of Connectedness: Social Media's False Promises — 31

Chapter 03: Connecting Across Landscapes: Technology's Impact on Social Bonds in Urban, Suburban, and Rural Areas — 43

Chapter 04: "The Psychology of Loneliness: Recognizing the Inner Signs — 57

Part II: The Irony of Technology-Induced Isolation

Chapter 05: When Phones Replace Humans: The Impact of Screen Time on Personal Relationships — 71

Chapter 06: The End of Privacy: How Constant Connectivity Can Create Distance — 85

Chapter 07: Echo Chambers and Filter Bubbles: Losing the Human Touch — 99

Part III: Technology as a Bridge, Not a Barrier

Chapter 08: Digital Tools for Real Connection: The Positive Side of Tech   113

Chapter 09: Fostering Community Online: Success Stories from the Virtual World   129

Chapter 10: The Future of Interaction: Innovations Bringing Us Closer   145

Part IV: Rebuilding Our Human Connections

Chapter 11: The Art of Mindful Technology Use: Creating Healthy Digital Habits   161

Chapter 12: From Online to Offline: Translating Digital Connections into Real-World Relationships   173

Chapter 13: Designing for Togetherness: How Developers Can Enhance Human Connection   187

Chapter 14: Spiritual Solace: Reconnecting with Self and Nature   201

Conclusion: Embracing Our Humanity in the Age of Technology - Reflecting on the lessons learned and envisioning a connected future   217

Footnotes   225

Bibliography   247

About The Author

Oreste J. DAversa (O-rest-ee DA-versa), CPC (Certified Professional Coach) is a Life Coach, Career/Job Search Coach, and College Major Coach **(www.CollegeMajorCoaching.com)**. He is the owner of Metropolitan Small Business Coaching LLC **(www.MetroSmallBusinessCoaching.com)** as a Business Coach, Consultant, and Trainer. He is an Inter-Faith (All-Faiths) Minister **(www.GodLovesYouAndMe.org)** ordained by *The New Seminary* in New York City, New York. He appears on podcasts, radio, and television programs discussing his expertise in business-related and personal development subjects.

He is the author of the following books:

- UNPLUGGED! A Practical Guide to Managing Teenage Stress in the Digital Age

- AI, Robots and Humans: Our Servants or Masters?

- Life Beyond the Pandemic: A Practical New Journey Handbook

- The Resume and Cover Letter Writing Toolkit for the Successful Job Seeker

- Power Interviewing: Proven Job Interview Techniques That Get You Results!

- The Step-by-Step Business Networking Kit: The Ultimate Business Networking System that Delivers Superior Results!

- SELL More Technology NOW!

- Selling for Non-Selling Professionals©

- Baby Boomer Entrepreneur: Implementing the Boomer Business Success System ®: The Complete and Proven Guide to Starting a Successful Business, having Financial Freedom with the Lifestyle that You Want

- Discovering Your Life Purpose: The Journey Within - The True Guide to Achieving Unlimited Happiness, Prosperity and Personal Fulfillment

- The Seven Simple Principles of Prosperity: Practical Exercises to Achieve a Rich, Happy and Joyous Life

- I Didn't Get a Chance to Say Good-bye ... Now What Can I Do?

- Write Your Own Funeral Service

- Healing the Holes in My Soul!: How I Saved My Own Life, Became Whole to Lead a Happy, Fulfilling and Joyous Life!

ACKNOWLEGEMENTS

In writing this book, I have traversed the complex terrain of loneliness in the digital age, and I have not walked this path alone. My journey has been illuminated by the wisdom, support, and encouragement of many remarkable individuals, to whom I am deeply grateful.

To the silent sufferers and the brave souls who yearn for genuine connection in a world that often feels increasingly distant – this book is for you. Your courage and vulnerability have been a profound source of inspiration and insight.

To my family and friends, thank you for your unwavering support and understanding. Your love and companionship have been my anchor, reminding me of the importance of real, face-to-face connections. You have been my constant reminder of what it means to truly connect.

To the researchers and academics whose work I have drawn upon, thank you for your rigorous investigations into the nature of human connection and technology's impact. Your contributions have provided a strong foundation for the discussions within this book.

A special thanks to the pioneers of digital tools and platforms that aim to bridge the gap between isolation and connection. Your innovative efforts offer hope and highlight the potential for technology to serve as a bridge rather than a barrier.

I am profoundly grateful to live in a country that gives me the opportunity to share my opinions with others without any type of political retaliation which has made it possible to bring these ideas to a wider audience, and for that, I am deeply thankful.

Lastly, to my readers: May this book serve as a beacon of hope and a guide toward meaningful connections. In our shared journey through the paradox of connection and isolation, know that you are not alone. Together, we can navigate the challenges of the digital age and rediscover the profound joy of human connection.

THIS PAGE INTENTIONALLY LEFT BLANK

PREFACE

Having spent and continuing to spend 80% of my life alone, partly by no fault of my own and partly by design, I understand that being alone can be both a blessing and a curse. The blessing is that you can live life, for the most part, on your own terms, and the curse part is that being alone for that length of time can cause you to think and do things that most people would never ever think of doing, let alone acting upon.

I have learned that spending this much time alone is not natural for us human beings and that all types of problems can and will arise when an individual spends this much time alone. Problems especially in the areas of mental and emotional well-being, which leads me to the reason why I wrote this book.

We are not taught how to be alone and to use this alone time to better ourselves as individuals. To increase our knowledge base, get to know ourselves better and to see how much we are really capable of becoming.

It is the purpose of this book, to help the reader become the limitless person that you have been created to become and to not fall into the various "rabbit-holes" of modern day society, especially by living your life behind an electronic screen.

Your life is meant to be lived to the fullest of your ability. May the information in this book help you become the person you are truly meant to be in this time and in this place. You need to "put the work in" to yourself and become the miracle "The Creator" has intended for you to become.

You'll have the knowledge, (with the tools in this book) learn them, implement them and go lead your best life – for yourself, your family, friends and humankind. You're here for a reason and a purpose, the sooner you start living your best life the sooner you'll be more happier, prosperous and joyful than you have ever been before!

Introduction: The Paradox of Connection and Isolation in the Digital Age

In today's hyper-connected world, the narrative of human interaction is being rewritten by the ubiquitous influence of technology. The phenomenon of sitting in a room full of people, all engrossed in their devices, is not merely a symbolic image but a stark reality that underscores a profound paradox: as the world grows more connected, why do so many of us feel all alone? **"Hey Humanity! Why Do I Feel All Alone in a World Full of People?"** explores this enigma, delving deep into how technology, while designed to connect us, has paradoxically also played a significant role in fostering a sense of isolation and loneliness.

This book begins a critical examination of the technological landscape that shapes our modern human connections. Through its pages, we unravel the complexity of our digital interactions and seek ways not only to mitigate the unintended consequences of these technological tools but also to leverage them in fostering genuine human connections.

The Advent of Digital Disconnection

As we explore this digital quandary, it becomes apparent that the tools created to bring us closer together—emails, instant messaging, social media—have instead layered a veneer of connection over an undercurrent of solitude. Each chapter in the book is designed to guide you through understanding this modern dilemma, from the evolution of human communication to the current state where digital interfaces often replace human touch.

Part I: Understanding Our Loneliness

We begin by tracing the evolution of communication. From the intimate face-to-face interactions that characterized early human societies to today's brief digital exchanges that often lack depth and emotional warmth, we explore how these shifts have influenced our social dynamics. The impact of social media is scrutinized—not just for its ability to create a facade of connectedness but also for its role in perpetuating feelings of isolation and inadequacy.

Moreover, we extend our analysis across various landscapes—urban, suburban, and rural—highlighting how technology influences social bonds differently in each setting. The psychological aspects of loneliness are dissected to understand the internal triggers that make us feel isolated even when we are, ostensibly, more connected than ever.

Part II: The Irony of Technology-Induced Isolation

The second part of the book delves into the ironies of technology-induced isolation. We discuss the peculiar situation where phones and screens replace human interactions, leading to a decline in the quality of personal relationships. The erosion of privacy and the rise of surveillance that comes with constant connectivity create distances—emotional and psychological—that are hard to bridge.

Furthermore, we explore the concept of "echo chambers" and "filter bubbles" that technology inadvertently supports—spaces where like-minded opinions are amplified, isolating us from diverse perspectives and further entrenching feelings of loneliness and division.

Part III: Technology as a Bridge, Not a Barrier

Contrary to the problems outlined, the third section of the book paints a more optimistic picture of technology. Here, we identify and discuss digital tools that have successfully fostered real connections. From platforms that unite communities online to the innovations that promise to bring us closer than ever before, this part focuses on the positive aspects of technology, showcasing stories and case studies where tech has effectively brought people together.

Part IV: Rebuilding Our Human Connections

In the final segment, we shift our focus from understanding and critique to action and healing. We discuss the art of mindful technology use, proposing strategies to cultivate healthier digital habits that can protect and enhance our real-world relationships. We also consider how online connections can be successfully translated into offline relationships and the role developers can play in designing technology that prioritizes human connection over mere interaction.

A new chapter on spiritual solace through meditation, creative visualization, and spending time in nature offers practical exercises and approaches for individuals to reconnect with themselves and the world around them, grounding their technological interactions in real-world experiences.

Embracing Our Humanity in the Age of Technology

This book does not merely lament the alienating effects of technology but provides a blueprint for how we can harness these powerful tools to enhance our human connections. It is a call to embrace our humanity with more consciousness in the age of technology, ensuring that we use these tools to truly enrich our lives and the lives of those around us.

Through this exploration, **"Hey Humanity! Why Do I Feel All Alone in a World Full of People?"** invites readers to rethink their relationship with technology, encouraging them to find a balance that fosters genuine connection and well-being. As we navigate this digital age, the lessons and strategies shared herein are more crucial than ever, providing the insights needed to transform our digital engagements into meaningful connections.

This introduction sets the stage for a deeper investigation into our digital lives and offers a compass for navigating the complexities of modern communication, urging us to forge paths that lead back to real connection and shared humanity.

THIS PAGE INTENTIONALLY LEFT BLANK

Chapter 01: The Evolution of Communication: From Face-to-Face to Digital Interfaces

In the beginning, communication was simple, direct, and face-to-face. The earliest humans relied on gestures, expressions, and vocalizations to convey their needs, emotions, and intentions. This form of communication was deeply rooted in our biology, engaging multiple senses and fostering strong social bonds. As societies evolved, so did our methods of communication, but it wasn't until the advent of technology that we saw a dramatic shift in how we connect with one another[1].

The Dawn of Language and Writing

Language emerged as a sophisticated tool that allowed humans to convey complex ideas, share stories, and build communities. Spoken language enabled us to express abstract concepts and emotions, creating a shared understanding that strengthened social ties[2]. As societies grew larger and more complex, the limitations of oral communication became apparent. Enter writing—the next significant leap in the evolution of communication.

Writing allowed information to be recorded, preserved, and disseminated across time and space. From the ancient

Sumerian cuneiform to Egyptian hieroglyphs and the Chinese script, writing systems evolved to meet the needs of diverse cultures[3]. These early forms of writing were primarily used for record-keeping, religious texts, and governance. The ability to document knowledge and experiences transformed societies, enabling the growth of civilizations and the sharing of wisdom across generations[4].

The Printing Press: A Revolution in Communication

The invention of the printing press in the 15th century by Johannes Gutenberg was a watershed moment in the history of communication[5]. This technological breakthrough democratized access to information, making books and other printed materials more affordable and widely available. The spread of literacy empowered individuals and facilitated the exchange of ideas, leading to cultural and intellectual revolutions such as The Renaissance and The Enlightenment (also known as the Age of Reason)[6].

The printing press also laid the foundation for the modern world by enabling the rise of newspapers, journals, and magazines. These publications played a crucial role in shaping public opinion, spreading news, and fostering a sense of community among readers[7]. The ability to reach a broad audience with written words transformed societies and set the stage for future advancements in communication technology[8].

The Telegraph and the Birth of Instant Communication

The 19th century saw the advent of the telegraph, which revolutionized long-distance communication[9]. For the first time in history, messages could be sent across vast distances almost instantaneously. Samuel Morse's invention of the Morse code and the development of telegraph networks enabled rapid communication between individuals, businesses, and governments[10]. The telegraph shrank the world, making it possible to connect with people in different cities, countries, and continents in real-time[11].

The impact of the telegraph on society was profound. It facilitated international trade, improved coordination in military operations, and brought people closer together by enabling instant communication[12]. However, it also marked the beginning of a shift away from face-to-face interactions, as people increasingly relied on technology to connect with others[13].

The Telephone: Bringing Voices to the Forefront

The invention of the telephone by Alexander Graham Bell in 1876 marked another significant milestone in the evolution of communication[14]. The telephone allowed people to hear each other's voices across distances, adding a personal touch to long-distance communication that the telegraph lacked. The ability to have real-time conversations over the phone bridged the gap between written correspondence and face-to-face interactions[15].

The telephone became a ubiquitous part of daily life, transforming how we connect with family, friends, and colleagues. It facilitated business transactions, enabled emergency services, and provided a means for maintaining personal relationships across distances[16]. Despite its many benefits, the telephone also contributed to the growing reliance on technology for communication, gradually reducing the frequency of in-person interactions[17].

The Digital Age: From Emails to Social Media

The late 20th and early 21st centuries witnessed the rise of digital communication technologies that have fundamentally altered how we interact with one another. The advent of the internet brought about a new era of connectivity, enabling people to communicate through emails, instant messaging, and online forums[18]. These digital platforms provided unprecedented convenience and speed, allowing for asynchronous communication that transcended time zones and geographical boundaries[19].

Email became a staple of professional and personal communication, offering a quick and efficient way to exchange information[20]. Instant messaging apps like AOL Instant Messenger and ICQ introduced real-time text-based conversations, fostering a sense of immediacy and intimacy[21]. Online forums and bulletin boards created virtual communities where people with shared interests could connect and exchange ideas[22].

The explosion of social media platforms in the 21st century, such as Facebook, Twitter, Instagram, and WhatsApp, further revolutionized digital communication[23]. Social media allowed people to share their lives, thoughts, and experiences with a global audience, creating a sense of connectedness and community. These platforms enabled real-time updates, multimedia sharing, and interactive engagement, making communication more dynamic and multifaceted[24].

The Double-Edged Sword of Digital Communication

While digital communication technologies have brought numerous benefits, they have also introduced challenges that contribute to feelings of loneliness and isolation. The convenience and efficiency of digital communication can sometimes come at the expense of deeper, more meaningful interactions[25]. The impersonal nature of text-based communication can lead to misunderstandings and a lack of emotional connection[26].

Social media, in particular, has been linked to increased feelings of loneliness and depression. The curated nature of social media profiles often creates unrealistic expectations and comparisons, leading to feelings of inadequacy and social isolation[27]. The constant bombardment of information and notifications can also contribute to stress and anxiety, making it difficult to disconnect and engage in face-to-face interactions[28].

Bridging the Gap: Using Technology to Foster Genuine Connections

Despite the challenges, technology also holds the potential to bring us closer together in meaningful ways. Video conferencing platforms like Zoom and Skype have made it possible to have face-to-face conversations with loved ones and colleagues, even when separated by great distances[29]. These tools have become especially important during times of crisis, such as the COVID-19 pandemic, when physical distancing measures limited in-person interactions[30].

Virtual Reality (VR) and Augmented Reality (AR) technologies are also paving the way for more immersive and interactive communication experiences. These technologies have the potential to create virtual environments that simulate face-to-face interactions, providing a sense of presence and connection that text-based communication lacks[31].

Furthermore, digital platforms can be used to foster communities and support networks. Online support groups, virtual meetups, and social media communities can provide a sense of belonging and connection for individuals who may feel isolated in their physical environments[32]. By leveraging technology thoughtfully and intentionally, we can use digital communication tools to enhance our relationships and build stronger, more connected communities[33].

The evolution of communication from face-to-face interactions to digital interfaces has transformed how we connect with one another. While technology has brought incredible advancements and conveniences, it has also introduced challenges that can contribute to feelings of loneliness and isolation[34]. By understanding the impact of these changes and finding ways to use technology to foster genuine connections, we can navigate the digital age in a way that brings us closer together as human beings[35].

Exercise: Navigating the Evolution of Communication

This exercise is designed to help you understand and implement the concepts discussed in Chapter 01: "The Evolution of Communication: From Face-to-Face to Digital Interfaces." It aims to encourage reflection on personal communication habits and the impact of technology on your social connections.

Step 1: Reflect on Your Communication Habits

Begin by examining your current communication habits. Answer the following questions to gain insight into how you interact with others:

1. Face-to-Face Interaction:

- How often do you engage in face-to-face conversations with family, friends, or colleagues?
- What types of face-to-face interactions do you find most fulfilling?

2. Digital Communication:

- How much time do you spend on digital communication platforms (e.g., email, social media, messaging apps) daily?
- Which digital communication tools do you use most frequently, and why?

3. Balance Between Digital and Face-to-Face Communication:

- Do you feel that digital communication has enhanced or hindered your ability to connect with others?

- How do you balance digital communication with face-to-face interactions?

Step 2: Identify Strengths and Weaknesses

Based on your reflections, identify the strengths and weaknesses of your current communication habits:

1. Strengths:

- List three aspects of your communication habits that you believe are effective and beneficial.
- Explain how these strengths contribute to your relationships and sense of connection.

2. Weaknesses:

- List three aspects of your communication habits that you find lacking or problematic.
- Describe how these weaknesses may be contributing to feelings of loneliness or disconnection.

Step 3: Set Personal Goals for Improved Communication

- Using the insights from your reflections, set two or three specific, achievable goals to improve your communication habits. Apply the **SMART** criteria

(**S**pecific, **M**easurable, **A**chievable, **R**elevant, **T**ime-bound) to formulate your goals.

Examples of Goals:

- *"I will have at least one face-to-face conversation with a friend or family member each week for the next month."*
- *"I will limit my social media usage to 30 minutes per day and use the extra time to engage in hobbies or social activities."*
- *"I will use video calls for my weekly check-ins with remote colleagues instead of relying solely on emails."*

Step 4: Develop an Action Plan

To achieve your goals, break them down into smaller, manageable tasks. These tasks should be practical steps you can take to improve your communication habits.

1. Goal: Increase Face-to-Face Conversations:

- **Task 1:** Schedule a weekly coffee date or walk with a friend or family member.
- **Task 2:** Join a local club or group that meets in person.
- **Task 3:** Organize a small gathering or dinner with loved ones.

2. Goal: Limit Social Media Usage:

- **Task 1:** Set a daily time limit on social media apps using built-in features on your phone.
- **Task 2:** Identify three alternative activities you can do instead of browsing social media (e.g., reading, exercising, volunteering).
- **Task 3:** Track your social media usage and alternative activities in a journal.

3. Goal: Use Video Calls for Remote Check-Ins:

- **Task 1:** Schedule regular video call meetings with remote colleagues or friends.
- **Task 2:** Prepare a list of topics or questions to discuss during the calls to ensure meaningful conversations.
- **Task 3:** Reflect on the quality of these interactions and adjust as needed.

Step 5: Monitor and Reflect on Progress

After implementing your action plan, take time to monitor and reflect on your progress:

1. Track Your Progress:

- Keep a journal or use an app to track your completion of tasks and overall progress towards your goals.
- Note any changes in your feelings of connectedness and loneliness.

2. Evaluate and Adjust:

- At the end of each week, evaluate the effectiveness of your action plan. Did you meet your goals? What challenges did you encounter?
- Adjust your goals and tasks as needed to better suit your needs and circumstances.

3. Seek Feedback:

- Ask for feedback from friends, family, or colleagues on any noticeable changes in your communication habits and relationships.

Use their insights to further refine your approach.

By engaging in this exercise, you can gain a deeper understanding of how the evolution of communication technologies has impacted your social connections.

Taking proactive steps to balance digital communication with face-to-face interactions can help you build stronger, more meaningful relationships. Remember, the key to effective communication is not just the medium used but the quality and intention behind each interaction.

NOTES:

Chapter 02: The Illusion of Connectedness: Social Media's False Promises

In an age where social media platforms dominate our daily lives, the promise of connectedness is tantalizing. We are constantly bombarded with images, messages, and updates that give the illusion of being closely knit with friends, family, and even strangers from across the globe. However, beneath this veneer of connectivity lies a paradox: despite being more "connected" than ever before, many of us feel more isolated, lonely, and disconnected from meaningful relationships.

The Allure of Social Media

Social media's allure is undeniable. Platforms like Facebook, Instagram, Twitter, and TikTok offer an endless stream of content that caters to our interests and preferences. The dopamine rush from likes, comments, and shares creates a cycle of dependency that keeps us coming back for more[1]. This constant engagement gives us a sense of belonging and validation, as if we are an integral part of a larger community.

Social media also provides an easy way to keep in touch with friends and family, no matter the distance. With just a few clicks, we can see photos of a cousin's wedding, watch a friend's vacation video, or read about a colleague's latest career achievement. This accessibility fosters a sense of closeness and immediacy that traditional forms of communication cannot match.

The Double-Edged Sword of Virtual Interaction

Despite these benefits, the interactions facilitated by social media are often superficial. A like on a photo or a brief comment on a status update does not equate to a deep, meaningful conversation. These interactions can give the illusion of closeness without the substance of true connection[2]. The brevity and public nature of social media exchanges often prevent us from engaging in the kind of vulnerable, intimate conversations that build strong relationships.

Moreover, social media encourages a form of performative interaction. We curate our online personas to present the best versions of ourselves, sharing highlights and successes while omitting struggles and failures[3]. This creates an environment where everyone seems to be living a perfect life, leading to comparisons that can diminish self-esteem and exacerbate feelings of inadequacy.

The Impact on Mental Health

Numerous studies have highlighted the negative impact of social media on mental health. Excessive use of social media has been linked to increased feelings of loneliness, depression, and anxiety[4]. The constant comparison with others' curated lives can lead to a distorted self-image and unrealistic expectations. Social media can also create a sense of FOMO (Fear Of Missing Out), where seeing others enjoy experiences we are not part of makes us feel left out and disconnected[5].

The addictive nature of social media can further exacerbate these issues. The need for constant validation and the fear of missing out can lead to compulsive checking of social media accounts, which disrupts real-life interactions and responsibilities. This can create a vicious cycle where the more we engage with social media, the more isolated and unhappy we feel[6].

The Paradox of Choice and Overwhelm

Social media platforms offer a dizzying array of choices in terms of content and interactions. While this abundance can be empowering, it can also be overwhelming. The paradox of choice suggests that having too many options can lead to decision paralysis and decreased satisfaction with our choices[6].

On social media, this translates to endless scrolling without meaningful engagement, leaving us feeling unsatisfied and disconnected.

Additionally, the sheer volume of information and stimuli on social media can be mentally exhausting. The constant barrage of updates, news, and notifications can lead to information overload, which can cause stress and anxiety[8]. This can make it difficult to focus on more meaningful, offline interactions and activities.

The Erosion of Privacy and Authenticity

Social media's pervasive nature has also eroded our sense of privacy. The pressure to share and document our lives can lead to oversharing and a loss of personal boundaries[9]. This can make it difficult to maintain a sense of authenticity and true self-expression, as we may feel compelled to conform to the norms and expectations of our online communities.

Moreover, the algorithms that drive social media platforms are designed to maximize engagement, often at the expense of our well-being[10]. These algorithms prioritize content that is sensational, controversial, or emotionally charged, which can skew our perceptions and foster negative emotions. This can create "echo chambers" where our views are constantly reinforced, leading to increased polarization and a diminished ability to engage in constructive, empathetic dialogue.

Finding Balance and Building Genuine Connections

While social media's promises of connectedness can be illusory, it is possible to use these platforms in ways that enhance our well-being and foster genuine connections. Here are some strategies to consider:

1. Limit Time Spent on Social Media: Set boundaries for how much time you spend on social media each day. Use tools like app timers or digital wellbeing features to monitor and limit your usage[11].

2. Curate Your Feed: Be intentional about the accounts you follow and the content you consume. Unfollow or mute accounts that make you feel negative or inadequate and seek out those that inspire and uplift you[12].

3. Engage Meaningfully: Focus on quality over quantity when it comes to interactions. Instead of passively scrolling and liking, take the time to leave thoughtful comments and engage in meaningful conversations[13].

4. Prioritize Offline Connections: Make a conscious effort to spend time with friends and family in person. Plan regular meetups, phone calls, or video chats to nurture your relationships[14].

5. Practice Digital Detoxes: Periodically take breaks from social media to recharge and reconnect with the offline world. Use this time to engage in activities that bring you joy and fulfillment[15].

6. Be Authentic: Strive to present an authentic version of yourself online. Share your successes and your struggles and encourage others to do the same. Authenticity fosters deeper connections and combats the pressure to present a perfect facade[16]..

Social media offers the promise of connectedness, but it often falls short of delivering meaningful, fulfilling relationships. The illusion of connectedness can lead to feelings of loneliness, inadequacy, and mental distress. By recognizing the limitations of social media and taking steps to use it mindfully, we can mitigate its negative effects and foster genuine connections that enhance our well-being. As we navigate the digital age, it is crucial to balance our online interactions with offline connections, ensuring that technology serves to bring us closer together rather than driving us apart.

Exercise: Finding Genuine Connection Beyond Social Media

This exercise is designed to help you understand and implement the concepts discussed in Chapter 02: "The Illusion of Connectedness: Social Media's False Promises." It aims to encourage reflection on your social media habits, identify areas for improvement, and foster genuine connections both online and offline.

Step 1: Reflect on Your Social Media Habits

Begin by examining your current social media usage. Answer the following questions to gain insight into how you interact with these platforms:

1. Daily Usage:

- How much time do you spend on social media each day?
- Which platforms do you use most frequently?

2. Types of Interactions:

- How often do you engage in meaningful conversations versus passive scrolling and liking?
- What types of content do you typically consume and share?

3. Emotional Impact:

- How do you feel after spending time on social media?

- Do you notice any patterns in your mood or self-esteem related to your social media usage?

Step 2: Identify Strengths and Weaknesses

Based on your reflections, identify the strengths and weaknesses of your current social media habits:

1. Strengths:

- List three positive aspects of your social media usage (e.g., staying in touch with distant friends, finding inspiration).
- Explain how these strengths contribute to your sense of connection and well-being.

2. Weaknesses:

- List three negative aspects of your social media usage (e.g., feeling inadequate, spending too much time online).
- Describe how these weaknesses may be contributing to feelings of loneliness or disconnection.

Step 3: Set Personal Goals for Balanced Social Media Use

Using the insights from your reflections, set two or three specific, achievable goals to improve your social media habits. Apply the **SMART** criteria (**S**pecific, **M**easurable, **A**chievable, **R**elevant, **T**ime-bound) to formulate your goals.

Examples of Goals:

- "I will limit my social media usage to 30 minutes per day and use an app timer to monitor this."
- "I will leave thoughtful comments on at least three posts per week instead of just liking them."
- "I will schedule a weekly phone call or video chat with a friend or family member."

Step 4: Develop an Action Plan

To achieve your goals, break them down into smaller, manageable tasks. These tasks should be practical steps you can take to improve your social media habits and foster genuine connections.

1. Goal: Limit Social Media Usage:

- **Task 1:** Set a daily time limit on your social media apps.
- **Task 2:** Identify three activities you can do instead of browsing social media (e.g., reading, exercising, spending time with loved ones).
- **Task 3:** Track your social media usage and alternative activities in a journal.

2. Goal: Engage Meaningfully:

- **Task 1:** Choose three friends or family members to regularly engage with on social media.

- **Task 2:** Leave thoughtful comments on their posts, asking questions or sharing insights.
- **Task 3:** Follow up with a direct message or call to deepen the conversation.

3. Goal: Prioritize Offline Connections:

- **Task 1:** Schedule a weekly meet-up, phone call, or video chat with a friend or family member.
- **Task 2:** Plan activities that allow for meaningful interaction, such as going for a walk, having a meal together, or participating in a shared hobby.
- **Task 3:** Reflect on these interactions in your journal, noting how they impact your feelings of connectedness.

Step 5: Monitor and Reflect on Progress

After implementing your action plan, take time to monitor and reflect on your progress:

1. Track Your Progress:

- Keep a journal or use an app to track your completion of tasks and overall progress towards your goals.
- Note any changes in your feelings of connectedness and loneliness.

2. Evaluate and Adjust:

- At the end of each week, evaluate the effectiveness of your action plan. Did you meet your goals? What challenges did you encounter?
- Adjust your goals and tasks as needed to better suit your needs and circumstances.

3. Seek Feedback:

- Ask for feedback from friends, family, or colleagues on any noticeable changes in your communication habits and relationships.
- Use their insights to further refine your approach.

Step 6: Practice Self-Compassion

Throughout this exercise, it's important to practice self-compassion. Acknowledge your efforts and be kind to yourself, especially if you encounter setbacks. Remember that building genuine connections and finding balance in social media usage takes time and patience.

Daily Self-Compassion Practice:

- Spend a few minutes each day reflecting on your accomplishments and what you're grateful for.
- Write positive affirmations that encourage and motivate you.

By engaging in this exercise, you can gain a deeper understanding of the illusion of connectedness that social media often creates and take concrete steps to foster genuine connections.

Balancing your online interactions with meaningful offline relationships can help reduce feelings of loneliness and enhance your overall well-being. Remember, the key to true connectedness lies in the quality of your interactions, both online and offline.

Chapter 03: Connecting Across Landscapes: Technology's Impact on Social Bonds in Urban, Suburban, and Rural Areas

The influence of technology on social bonds varies widely across different geographic landscapes. Urban, suburban, and rural areas each present unique contexts and challenges that shape how technology impacts our connections with others. Understanding these differences is crucial to addressing the feelings of loneliness and disconnection that many people experience in our technologically driven world.

Urban Areas: The Paradox of Proximity

Urban areas are characterized by high population density and a fast-paced lifestyle. Cities offer a plethora of opportunities for social interaction, yet urban residents often report high levels of loneliness and social isolation[1].

The Role of Technology

In cities, technology serves as both a bridge and a barrier to social connections. Social media, messaging apps, and dating platforms provide convenient ways to meet new people and maintain relationships amidst busy schedules. These tools can help urban dwellers find community in a sea of strangers, offering a sense of belonging and connection[2].

However, the same technology can also exacerbate feelings of isolation. The anonymity of urban life, combined with the superficial nature of many online interactions, can lead to a lack of deep, meaningful relationships[3]. Moreover, the constant stimulation and noise of city living can make it challenging to disconnect and engage in face-to-face interactions, further weakening social bonds[4].

Suburban Areas: Bridging Physical and Digital Gaps

Suburban areas, with their lower density and more spread-out communities, offer a different set of social dynamics. Suburban life often centers around family and close-knit communities, but can also lead to feelings of isolation, particularly for those who are not integrated into these social structures[5].

The Role of Technology

For suburban residents, technology can help bridge the physical gaps that come with living in more spread-out environments. Social media platforms, community forums, and neighborhood apps like Nextdoor facilitate local connections and community engagement[6]. These tools can help residents stay informed about local events, share resources, and build a sense of community.

However, the reliance on digital communication in suburban areas can also lead to a decline in face-to-face interactions. While online platforms make it easier to connect, they can also create a false sense of community, where online interactions replace more meaningful, in-person relationships[7]. Additionally, the privacy and isolation of suburban living can sometimes discourage the spontaneous social interactions that are more common in urban areas[8].

Rural Areas: Overcoming Distance with Digital Connectivity

Rural areas are often characterized by low population density and greater physical distances between residents. These factors can contribute to social isolation, as opportunities for social interaction are more limited compared to urban and suburban settings[9].

The Role of Technology

In rural areas, technology plays a critical role in overcoming the challenges of physical distance. Internet access, though sometimes limited, allows rural residents to connect with friends and family, access educational resources, and participate in online communities[10]. Social media and video conferencing tools like Skype and Zoom are particularly valuable for maintaining social bonds and reducing feelings of isolation.

Despite these benefits, the digital divide remains a significant issue in rural areas. Limited access to high-speed internet and digital literacy can hinder the ability of rural residents to fully engage with online platforms and resources[11]. This gap can exacerbate feelings of isolation and exclusion, particularly for older adults and those with limited technological skills[12].

Common Challenges and Opportunities

Across urban, suburban, and rural areas, several common challenges and opportunities emerge in the context of technology and social bonds.

Challenges

1. Superficial Connections: Technology often facilitates quick, surface-level interactions rather than deep, meaningful relationships. This can lead to a sense of emptiness and dissatisfaction with social connections[13].

2. Digital Divide: Access to technology and digital literacy vary widely, impacting the ability of individuals to connect and engage online. This divide is particularly pronounced in rural areas and among older adults[14].

3, Privacy Concerns: The pervasive nature of technology raises concerns about privacy and the potential for oversharing. Maintaining boundaries and authenticity online can be challenging[15].

Opportunities

1. Enhanced Connectivity: Technology provides unprecedented opportunities for connecting with others, regardless of physical distance. This is particularly beneficial in rural areas where social opportunities are limited[16].

2. Community Building: Online platforms can foster community engagement and collective action. Tools like neighborhood apps and social media groups can enhance local connections and support networks[17].

3. Support Networks: Technology enables the creation of virtual support networks for individuals facing similar challenges. Online groups and forums can provide emotional support, information, and a sense of belonging[18].

Strategies for Strengthening Social Bonds

To mitigate the negative impacts of technology on social bonds and enhance its positive effects, consider the following strategies:

1. Balance Online and Offline Interactions: Make a conscious effort to balance online interactions with face-to-face communication. Prioritize in-person meetings and gatherings to build deeper, more meaningful relationships[19].

2. Promote Digital Literacy: Advocate for improved digital literacy and access to technology, particularly in rural areas. This can help bridge the digital divide and ensure that everyone can benefit from the opportunities that technology offers[20].

3. Encourage Authenticity: Foster authentic interactions online by sharing both successes and challenges. Encourage others to do the same, creating a more genuine and supportive digital environment[21].

4. Leverage Technology for Community Building: Use technology to enhance local community engagement. Participate in neighborhood apps, local social media groups, and online forums that focus on local issues and events[22].

5. Create Support Networks: Utilize online platforms to create and join support networks. These can provide valuable emotional support and resources, particularly for those who feel isolated or marginalized[23].

The impact of technology on social bonds varies across urban, suburban, and rural areas, reflecting the unique challenges and opportunities of each landscape. By understanding these dynamics and adopting strategies to promote meaningful connections, we can harness the power of technology to enhance our social bonds and reduce feelings of loneliness and isolation. As we navigate the digital age, it is essential to find a balance that allows us to connect deeply and authentically with others, regardless of where we live.

Exercise: Strengthening Social Bonds Across Different Landscapes

This exercise is designed to help you understand and implement the concepts discussed in Chapter 03: "Connecting Across Landscapes: Technology's Impact on Social Bonds in Urban, Suburban, and Rural Areas." It aims to encourage reflection on your use of technology in fostering social connections and to create actionable steps to improve your social bonds.

Step 1: Reflect on Your Social Environment

Begin by examining your current social environment and the role technology plays in your interactions. Answer the following questions to gain insight into your social bonds:

1. Geographic Landscape:

- Do you live in an urban, suburban, or rural area?
- What are the unique social dynamics and challenges of your environment?

2. Technology Usage:

- How do you use technology to connect with others (e.g., social media, messaging apps, video calls)?
- How effective do you find these tools in maintaining meaningful relationships?

3. Balance of Interactions:

- How do you balance online interactions with face-to-face communication?
- What challenges do you face in achieving this balance?

Step 2: Identify Strengths and Weaknesses

Based on your reflections, identify the strengths and weaknesses of your current social bonds and technology usage:

1. **Strengths:**

    - List three positive aspects of your social interactions and how technology supports them.
    - Explain how these strengths contribute to your sense of connection and community.

2. **Weaknesses:**

    - List three negative aspects of your social interactions and how technology might be hindering them.
    - Describe how these weaknesses may be contributing to feelings of loneliness or disconnection.

Step 3: Set Personal Goals for Enhanced Social Bonds

Using the insights from your reflections, set two or three specific, achievable goals to improve your social bonds. Apply the **SMART** criteria (**S**pecific, **M**easurable, **A**chievable, **R**elevant, **T**ime-bound) to formulate your goals.

Examples of Goals:

- *"I will schedule a weekly in-person meetup with friends or family for the next three months."*

- *"I will reduce my daily social media usage to one hour and use the extra time to engage in local community activities."*
- *"I will join a neighborhood app and participate in local events to build a stronger sense of community."*

Step 4: Develop an Action Plan

To achieve your goals, break them down into smaller, manageable tasks. These tasks should be practical steps you can take to improve your social interactions and foster meaningful connections.

1. Goal: Schedule Weekly In-Person Meetups:

- **Task 1:** Identify friends or family members you want to reconnect with.
- **Task 2:** Reach out to them to propose a regular meetup schedule.
- **Task 3:** Plan activities for these meetups that encourage meaningful interaction, such as shared hobbies or outings.

2. Goal: Reduce Social Media Usage:

- **Task 1:** Set daily time limits on your social media apps.

- **Task 2:** Identify alternative activities to fill the time, such as reading, exercising, or volunteering.
- **Task 3:** Track your social media usage and alternative activities in a journal.

3. Goal: Participate in Local Community Activities:

- **Task 1:** Join a neighborhood app or local social media group.
- **Task 2:** Look for local events or community groups that match your interests.
- **Task 3:** Attend at least one local event or meeting each week and engage with other participants.

Step 5: Monitor and Reflect on Progress

After implementing your action plan, take time to monitor and reflect on your progress:

1. Track Your Progress:

- Keep a journal or use an app to track your completion of tasks and overall progress towards your goals.
- Note any changes in your feelings of connectedness and loneliness.

2. Evaluate and Adjust:

- At the end of each week, evaluate the effectiveness of your action plan. Did you meet your goals? What challenges did you encounter?
- Adjust your goals and tasks as needed to better suit your needs and circumstances.

3. Seek Feedback:

- Ask for feedback from friends, family, or community members on any noticeable changes in your communication habits and relationships.
- Use their insights to further refine your approach.

Step 6: Foster Authenticity and Digital Literacy

Throughout this exercise, it's important to foster authenticity in your interactions and improve your digital literacy:

1. Authenticity:

- Share both your successes and challenges with others, both online and offline.
- Encourage genuine, supportive interactions by being open and honest.

2. Digital Literacy:

- Take steps to improve your understanding of digital tools and platforms.
- Advocate for digital literacy initiatives in your community to help bridge the digital divide.

By engaging in this exercise, you can gain a deeper understanding of how technology impacts your social bonds across different landscapes. Taking proactive steps to balance online and offline interactions, foster authenticity, and improve digital literacy can help you build stronger, more meaningful connections. Remember, the key to reducing feelings of loneliness and enhancing your well-being lies in the quality of your social interactions and the genuine connections you create, regardless of where you live.

NOTES:

Chapter 04: The Psychology of Loneliness: Recognizing the Inner Signs

Loneliness is a universal human experience, yet it is deeply personal and often misunderstood. It goes beyond mere physical isolation, tapping into our emotional and psychological states. Understanding the psychology of loneliness is crucial to recognizing the inner signs and addressing the underlying issues that contribute to this pervasive feeling. This chapter delves into the psychological aspects of loneliness, offering insights into how it manifests and how we can begin to address it.

The Nature of Loneliness

Loneliness is often described as a subjective feeling of isolation, where a person feels disconnected from others despite being surrounded by people[1]. This sense of disconnection can be profoundly distressing and can impact both mental and physical health. It is important to distinguish between loneliness and solitude; while solitude is the voluntary choice to be alone, loneliness is a state of being that feels imposed and unwanted.

The Psychological Roots of Loneliness

Several psychological factors contribute to feelings of loneliness. These include:

1. Social Anxiety: Individuals with social anxiety often experience intense fear and discomfort in social situations, leading to avoidance behaviors that can result in isolation[2]. The fear of negative evaluation and rejection makes it difficult for them to form and maintain relationships.

2. Low Self-Esteem: People with low self-esteem may believe they are unworthy of love and friendship, which can prevent them from reaching out to others[3]. This negative self-perception can create a self-fulfilling prophecy where their expectations of rejection lead to actual social withdrawal.

3. Attachment Styles: Early childhood experiences with caregivers shape our attachment styles, which influence how we relate to others throughout our lives[4]. Those with insecure attachment styles, such as anxious or avoidant attachment, may struggle with forming healthy, lasting relationships.

4. Life Transitions: Major life changes, such as moving to a new city, starting a new job, or experiencing the loss of a loved one, can disrupt social networks and contribute to feelings of loneliness[5]. These transitions often require significant emotional adjustment and can leave individuals feeling vulnerable and isolated.

Recognizing the Inner Signs of Loneliness

Identifying the inner signs of loneliness is the first step toward addressing it. Some common psychological and emotional indicators include:

1. Persistent Sadness: Chronic loneliness is often accompanied by feelings of sadness and despair. This persistent low mood can make it difficult to find joy in everyday activities[6].

2. Lack of Motivation: Loneliness can sap one's energy and motivation, leading to a lack of interest in activities that were once enjoyable[7]. This can create a cycle where decreased activity leads to further isolation and loneliness.

3. Negative Thought Patterns: Individuals experiencing loneliness often engage in negative self-talk and ruminate on their perceived inadequacies[8]. This can exacerbate feelings of worthlessness and further isolate them from potential social interactions.

4. Heightened Sensitivity: Lonely individuals may become hypersensitive to social cues and perceive rejection or criticism even when it is not present[9]. This heightened sensitivity can make social interactions more stressful and challenging.

5. Physical Symptoms: Loneliness can manifest physically through symptoms such as headaches, gastrointestinal issues, and disrupted sleep patterns[10]. These physical signs can further impact one's overall well-being and contribute to a cycle of distress.

The Impact of Loneliness on Mental Health

The psychological effects of loneliness are profound and far-reaching. Chronic loneliness is linked to a range of mental health issues, including:

1. Depression: Loneliness is a significant risk factor for depression. The persistent feeling of being alone and disconnected can lead to depressive symptoms, such as prolonged sadness, hopelessness, and a lack of interest in life[11].

2. Anxiety: In addition to social anxiety, chronic loneliness can contribute to generalized anxiety. The constant worry about social interactions and the fear of being alone can create a pervasive sense of unease[12].

3. Cognitive Decline: Research has shown that loneliness can negatively impact cognitive function, leading to memory problems and impaired executive function[13]. This cognitive decline can further isolate individuals and make it more difficult to engage in social activities.

Strategies for Addressing Loneliness

Recognizing the inner signs of loneliness is crucial, but taking action to address it is equally important. Here are some strategies to combat loneliness:

1. Foster Connections: Making an effort to connect with others, even in small ways, can help reduce feelings of loneliness. This can include reaching out to friends and family, joining social groups, or participating in community activities[14].

2. Seek Professional Help: Therapy can be a valuable tool for addressing the underlying psychological factors contributing to loneliness. Cognitive-behavioral therapy (CBT) and other therapeutic approaches can help individuals challenge negative thought patterns and develop healthier coping mechanisms[15].

3. Practice Self-Compassion: Being kind to oneself and practicing self-compassion can counteract the negative self-talk that often accompanies loneliness[16]. Self-compassion involves treating oneself with the same kindness and understanding that one would offer a friend.

4. Engage in Meaningful Activities: Finding activities that provide a sense of purpose and fulfillment can help combat loneliness. This can include volunteering, pursuing hobbies, or engaging in creative pursuits[17]. Meaningful activities can provide opportunities for social interaction and help individuals feel more connected to their communities.

5. Utilize Technology Wisely: While technology can sometimes exacerbate feelings of loneliness, it can also be a valuable tool for connection. Using social media, video calls, and online communities mindfully can help maintain and strengthen relationships[18].

Loneliness is a complex and multifaceted experience that affects individuals on a deep psychological level. By recognizing the inner signs of loneliness and understanding its psychological roots, we can take steps to address it effectively. Whether through fostering connections, seeking professional help, or engaging in meaningful activities, it is possible to overcome loneliness and build a more fulfilling, connected life. As we navigate the challenges of a digitally connected world, it is essential to prioritize genuine human connection and emotional well-being.

Exercise: Recognizing and Addressing the Inner Signs of Loneliness

This exercise is designed to help you understand and implement the concepts discussed in Chapter 04: "The Psychology of Loneliness: Recognizing the Inner Signs." It aims to encourage self-reflection, identify signs of loneliness, and create actionable steps to address and mitigate feelings of isolation.

Step 1: Self-Reflection

Begin by reflecting on your current emotional and psychological state. Answer the following questions to gain insight into your feelings of loneliness:

1. Emotional State:

- How often do you feel lonely or isolated?
- What specific situations trigger these feelings?

2. Physical Symptoms:

- Do you experience physical symptoms such as headaches, gastrointestinal issues, or disrupted sleep when feeling lonely?
- How do these physical symptoms affect your daily life?

3. Social Interactions:

- How often do you engage in meaningful conversations with friends, family, or colleagues?
- Do you find it difficult to initiate or maintain social interactions?

Step 2: Identify the Inner Signs of Loneliness

Based on your reflections, identify the specific signs of loneliness you experience. Use the following checklist to recognize common psychological and emotional indicators:

1. Persistent Sadness:

- Do you often feel sad or despairing?
- Is this sadness affecting your ability to enjoy daily activities?

2. Lack of Motivation:

- Do you feel a lack of energy or motivation to participate in activities you once enjoyed?
- Has this led to further isolation?

3. Negative Thought Patterns:

- Do you engage in negative self-talk or ruminate on perceived inadequacies?
- How do these thought patterns affect your self-esteem and social interactions?

4. Heightened Sensitivity:

- Are you hypersensitive to social cues, perceiving rejection or criticism even when it may not be present?
- How does this sensitivity impact your social interactions?

Step 3: Set Personal Goals for Addressing Loneliness

Using the insights from your reflections, set two or three specific, achievable goals to address your feelings of loneliness. Apply the **SMART** criteria (**S**pecific, **M**easurable, **A**chievable, **R**elevant, **T**ime-bound) to formulate your goals.

Examples of Goals:

- *"I will reach out to one friend or family member each week for a meaningful conversation."*
- *"I will join a local hobby group or community activity within the next month."*

- *"I will practice self-compassion daily by writing positive affirmations in a journal."*

Step 4: Develop an Action Plan

To achieve your goals, break them down into smaller, manageable tasks. These tasks should be practical steps you can take to address and mitigate feelings of loneliness.

1. Goal: Reach Out for Meaningful Conversations:

- **Task 1:** Make a list of friends and family members you feel comfortable reaching out to.
- **Task 2:** Schedule a specific time each week to call or meet with one person on your list.
- **Task 3:** Prepare a few conversation topics or questions to ensure a meaningful discussion.

2. Goal: Join a Local Hobby Group:

- **Task 1:** Research local hobby groups or community activities that interest you.
- **Task 2:** Contact the group organizer to inquire about joining.
- **Task 3:** Attend the next scheduled meeting or event and actively participate.

3. Goal: Practice Self-Compassion:

- **Task 1:** Write down three positive affirmations to say to yourself each day.
- **Task 2:** Spend a few minutes each day reflecting on your accomplishments and what you are grateful for.
- **Task 3:** Treat yourself with kindness and understanding, especially during challenging times.

Step 5: Monitor and Reflect on Progress

After implementing your action plan, take time to monitor and reflect on your progress:

1. Track Your Progress:

- Keep a journal to track your completion of tasks and overall progress towards your goals.
- Note any changes in your feelings of connectedness and loneliness.

2. Evaluate and Adjust:

- At the end of each week, evaluate the effectiveness of your action plan. Did you meet your goals? What challenges did you encounter?

- Adjust your goals and tasks as needed to better suit your needs and circumstances.

3. Seek Feedback:

- Ask for feedback from friends, family, or a therapist on any noticeable changes in your emotional well-being and social interactions.
- Use their insights to further refine your approach.

Step 6: Foster Genuine Connections and Emotional Well-Being

Throughout this exercise, it's important to foster genuine connections and prioritize your emotional well-being:

1. Foster Connections:

- Make a conscious effort to connect with others in meaningful ways, both online and offline.
- Participate in community activities and social groups that align with your interests.

2. Prioritize Emotional Well-Being:

- Practice self-compassion and self-care regularly.
- Seek professional help if needed to address underlying psychological factors contributing to loneliness.

By engaging in this exercise, you can gain a deeper understanding of the inner signs of loneliness and take proactive steps to address and mitigate these feelings. Building meaningful connections, practicing self-compassion, and engaging in activities that bring you joy can help you overcome loneliness and build a more fulfilling, connected life. Remember, the key to addressing loneliness lies in recognizing the inner signs and taking actionable steps towards genuine human connection and emotional well-being.

NOTES:

Chapter 05: When Phones Replace Humans: The Impact of Screen Time on Personal Relationships

In today's world, our smartphones have become indispensable tools. They connect us to information, entertainment, and each other in ways that were unimaginable just a few decades ago. Yet, as these devices have become integral to our daily lives, they have also begun to replace genuine human interaction, often at the expense of our personal relationships. This chapter explores the impact of screen time on our connections with others and offers insights into how we can reclaim the depth and quality of our relationships in the age of digital distraction.

The Ubiquity of Smartphones

The smartphone is arguably one of the most transformative inventions of the 21st century. With the touch of a button, we can access a world of information, connect with people across the globe, and entertain ourselves in countless ways. However, this constant connectivity comes with a cost. The average person spends several hours a day on their phone, often at the expense of face-to-face interactions with those around them[1].

The Double-Edged Sword of Connectivity

While smartphones enable us to stay in touch with distant friends and family, they can also create a paradoxical sense of isolation. The constant barrage of notifications and the pressure to stay connected can lead to superficial interactions and a lack of meaningful engagement. This phenomenon, often referred to as "Phubbing" (phone snubbing), occurs when individuals pay more attention to their phones than to the people they are physically present with[2].

The Psychological Impact of Phubbing

Phubbing can have significant psychological effects on both the phubber and the person being phubbed. For the person being ignored, it can lead to feelings of rejection, devaluation, and loneliness[3]. Studies have shown that phubbing can undermine relationship satisfaction and increase feelings of depression and anxiety[4]. For the phubber, the constant need to check their phone can create a cycle of distraction and disconnection, preventing them from fully engaging in the present moment and fostering deep, meaningful relationships[5].

Screen Time and Relationship Quality

The overuse of smartphones and other digital devices can erode the quality of our personal relationships in several ways:

1. Reduced Attention and Presence: Being glued to our screens means we are often only partially present in our interactions with others. This divided attention can hinder effective communication and reduce the emotional intimacy that is crucial for strong relationships[6].

2. Decreased Empathy: The more time we spend interacting through screens, the less we engage in face-to-face conversations where non-verbal cues and emotional expressions play a key role. This can lead to a decline in our ability to empathize and connect emotionally with others[7].

3. Increased Conflict: The presence of smartphones during social interactions can be a source of tension and conflict. Partners, friends, and family members may feel neglected or undervalued when their loved ones prioritize their devices over their relationship[8].

4. Sleep Disruption: Excessive screen time, especially before bed, can disrupt sleep patterns, leading to fatigue and irritability. Poor sleep can negatively impact our mood and our ability to engage positively with others[9].

The Impact on Romantic Relationships

Romantic relationships are particularly vulnerable to the effects of excessive screen time. The constant presence of smartphones can create a barrier to intimacy and connection. Partners may feel that their significant other is more interested in their phone than in their relationship, leading to feelings of neglect and resentment[10].

Strategies for Reclaiming Relationship Quality

Recognizing the impact of screen time on our personal relationships is the first step toward making positive changes. Here are some strategies to help reclaim the depth and quality of your relationships in the age of digital distraction:

1. Set Boundaries for Screen Time: Establish clear boundaries for when and where you use your smartphone. For example, designate specific times of the day as phone-free, such as during meals, date nights, or family gatherings[11].

2. Prioritize Face-to-Face Interactions: Make a conscious effort to engage in face-to-face conversations and activities. This can help strengthen your emotional connection and improve communication[12].

3. Practice Mindfulness: Mindfulness can help you stay present and fully engage in your interactions with others. Put your phone away and focus on the person you are with, giving them your full attention[13].

4. Create Tech-Free Zones: Designate certain areas of your home as tech-free zones, such as the dining room or bedroom. This can help reduce distractions and promote more meaningful interactions[14].

5. Communicate Openly: Discuss your screen time habits with your loved ones and agree on mutual expectations for device use. Open communication can help prevent misunderstandings and foster a supportive environment[15].

6. Use Technology Wisely: Leverage technology to enhance, rather than replace, your relationships. Use video calls to stay connected with distant friends and family, but don't let these interactions replace in-person meetings when possible[16].

The Role of Self-Awareness

Self-awareness is key to managing screen time effectively. Reflect on your own habits and consider how they may be affecting your relationships. Are you guilty of phubbing? Do you find it difficult to disconnect from your phone? By acknowledging these patterns, you can take proactive steps to make positive changes[17].

Building a Balanced Digital Life

Achieving a balanced digital life is about finding harmony between technology use and human connection. It's not about completely eliminating screen time, but rather about using it in a way that supports and enhances your relationships. Here are some tips to help you build a balanced digital life:

1. Be Intentional: Use your smartphone with intention, rather than out of habit or boredom. Ask yourself whether checking your phone in a given moment will add value to your life or detract from it[18].

2. Engage in Offline Activities: Find activities that you enjoy that do not involve screens, such as reading, exercising, or spending time in nature. These activities can help you recharge and provide opportunities for meaningful interactions[19].

3. Limit Social Media Use: Social media can be a major time drain and source of distraction. Set limits on your social media use and focus on engaging with people in person[20].

4. Foster Real Connections: Make an effort to build and maintain real-life connections. Join clubs, attend events, and participate in community activities to meet new people and strengthen existing relationships[21].

In an era where smartphones and digital devices are ubiquitous, it's easy to let screen time replace human interaction. However, the quality of our personal relationships depends on our ability to connect deeply and authentically with others. By setting boundaries, practicing mindfulness, and prioritizing face-to-face interactions, we can mitigate the negative impact of screen time and foster stronger, more meaningful relationships. As we navigate the digital age, let us remember that while technology can connect us, it is our human connections that truly enrich our lives.

Exercise: Reducing Screen Time to Enhance Personal Relationships

This exercise is designed to help you understand and implement the concepts discussed in Chapter 05: "When Phones Replace Humans: The Impact of Screen Time on Personal Relationships." It aims to encourage self-reflection, create awareness of screen time habits, and develop actionable steps to improve your relationships by reducing screen time and enhancing face-to-face interactions.

Step 1: Self-Reflection

Begin by reflecting on your current screen time habits and their impact on your personal relationships. Answer the following questions to gain insight into your behaviors and feelings:

1. Screen Time Awareness:
- How many hours per day do you spend on your smartphone?
- What are the primary activities you engage in on your phone (e.g., social media, messaging, gaming)?

2. Impact on Relationships:

- How do you feel your screen time affects your relationships with family, friends, and romantic partners?
- Have you ever experienced conflicts or feelings of neglect due to smartphone use?

3. Personal Feelings:

- Do you often feel distracted or disconnected during face-to-face interactions?
- How do you feel after spending a significant amount of time on your phone?

Step 2: Identify Strengths and Weaknesses

Based on your reflections, identify the strengths and weaknesses of your current screen time habits:

1. **Strengths:**

   - List three positive aspects of your smartphone use (e.g., staying connected with distant family, accessing information quickly).
   - Explain how these strengths contribute to your daily life and relationships.

2. **Weaknesses:**

   - List three negative aspects of your smartphone use (e.g., feeling disconnected during conversations, neglecting face-to-face interactions).
   - Describe how these weaknesses may be contributing to feelings of isolation or relationship strain.

Step 3: Set Personal Goals for Reducing Screen Time

Using the insights from your reflections, set two or three specific, achievable goals to reduce your screen time and enhance your personal relationships. Apply the **SMART** criteria (**S**pecific, **M**easurable, **A**chievable, **R**elevant, **T**ime-bound) to formulate your goals.

Examples of Goals:

- *"I will reduce my social media usage to 30 minutes per day and use the saved time to engage in face-to-face conversations with family members."*
- *"I will have at least one phone-free meal with my family every day."*
- *"I will practice mindfulness by putting my phone away during all face-to-face interactions for the next month."*

Step 4: Develop an Action Plan

To achieve your goals, break them down into smaller, manageable tasks. These tasks should be practical steps you can take to reduce screen time and improve your relationships.

1. Goal: Reduce Social Media Usage:

- **Task 1:** Set a daily time limit on your social media apps using built-in features on your phone.
- **Task 2:** Identify alternative activities to fill the time, such as reading, exercising, or spending time with loved ones.
- **Task 3:** Track your social media usage and alternative activities in a journal.

2. Goal: Have Phone-Free Meals:

- **Task 1:** Designate specific times and locations for phone-free meals (e.g., dining room, breakfast time).
- **Task 2:** Communicate this goal to your family and encourage them to participate.
- **Task 3:** Reflect on the quality of your interactions during these meals in your journal.

3. Goal: Practice Mindfulness:

- **Task 1:** Set reminders to put your phone away during face-to-face interactions.
- **Task 2:** Practice being fully present by focusing on the conversation and avoiding distractions.
- **Task 3:** Reflect on your experiences and any improvements in your relationships.

Step 5: Monitor and Reflect on Progress

After implementing your action plan, take time to monitor and reflect on your progress:

1. Track Your Progress:

- Keep a journal or use an app to track your completion of tasks and overall progress towards your goals.

- Note any changes in your feelings of connectedness and relationship satisfaction.

2. Evaluate and Adjust:

- At the end of each week, evaluate the effectiveness of your action plan. Did you meet your goals? What challenges did you encounter?
- Adjust your goals and tasks as needed to better suit your needs and circumstances.

3. Seek Feedback:

- Ask for feedback from friends, family, or romantic partners on any noticeable changes in your interactions and relationship quality.
- Use their insights to further refine your approach.

Step 6: Foster Long-Term Changes

To ensure lasting improvements in your relationships and screen time habits, consider the following strategies:

1. Create Lasting Habits:

- Turn successful tasks into long-term habits by integrating them into your daily routine.

- Continuously practice mindfulness and intentional screen use to maintain a balanced digital life.

2. Stay Accountable:

- Share your goals and progress with a trusted friend or family member who can help keep you accountable.
- Regularly review and adjust your goals to stay on track.

3. Celebrate Progress:

- Celebrate your successes and progress, no matter how small. Acknowledge the positive impact these changes have on your relationships.

By engaging in this exercise, you can gain a deeper understanding of how screen time impacts your personal relationships and take proactive steps to reduce its negative effects. Setting boundaries, practicing mindfulness, and prioritizing face-to-face interactions can help you build stronger, more meaningful connections with those around you. Remember, the key to enhancing your relationships lies in finding a balance between digital convenience and genuine human connection.

NOTES:

Chapter 06: The End of Privacy: How Constant Connectivity Can Create Distance

In an age where technology allows for constant connectivity, the concept of privacy has become increasingly elusive. The pervasive presence of social media, smartphones, and the internet has created a culture where sharing our lives publicly is not only common but often expected. While this connectivity promises to bring us closer together, it paradoxically can create distance and feelings of disconnection. This chapter explores the impact of constant connectivity on privacy and how it can lead to emotional and social distancing.

The Erosion of Privacy in the Digital Age

Privacy used to be a cornerstone of personal life. It allowed individuals to maintain boundaries and control over their personal information. However, with the advent of social media and digital communication, the lines between private and public life have blurred. Today, many aspects of our lives are documented and shared online, from personal milestones to daily activities[1].

The Pressure to Share

Social media platforms thrive on sharing. They encourage users to post updates, photos, and videos, often rewarding frequent sharing with likes, comments, and followers. This creates a pressure to share more of our personal lives online, leading to the erosion of privacy. The need for validation and approval from online connections can drive individuals to disclose more than they are comfortable with, making privacy a rare commodity[2].

The Impact on Personal Relationships

Constant connectivity and the lack of privacy can significantly impact personal relationships. The pressure to maintain an online presence can lead to superficial interactions and a lack of genuine connection. Here are some ways in which the end of privacy can create distance:

Superficial Connections

Social media fosters an environment of superficial connections. The interactions that take place online are often brief and lack depth. A like or a comment on a post cannot replace a meaningful, in-person conversation. This superficiality can make relationships feel shallow and unsatisfying, leading to feelings of loneliness and disconnection[3].

The Illusion of Intimacy

Sharing personal details online can create an illusion of intimacy. Followers and friends on social media may feel they know someone well based on their posts, but this perceived intimacy is often misleading. The curated nature of social media profiles means that only selective aspects of a person's life are shared, leaving out the full spectrum of experiences and emotions. This can create a false sense of closeness that does not translate into real-life emotional support and understanding[4].

Digital Surveillance

The constant sharing of personal information can also lead to a sense of being watched or surveilled. Knowing that our actions and words are constantly being observed by an online audience can make individuals feel exposed and vulnerable. This awareness can inhibit authentic self-expression and lead to self-censorship, further distancing us from genuine interactions[5].

The Psychological Toll

The erosion of privacy and constant connectivity can take a significant psychological toll. The pressure to maintain an online presence and the resulting superficial interactions can lead to increased stress and anxiety. Here are some of the psychological impacts:

Fear of Missing Out (FOMO)

Constant connectivity can exacerbate the Fear Of Missing Out (FOMO). Seeing others' highlight reels on social media can create a sense of inadequacy and envy, making individuals feel as though they are missing out on experiences and connections. This can lead to increased anxiety and a relentless need to stay connected, further eroding privacy and personal boundaries[6].

Comparison and Self-Esteem

Social media platforms often promote comparison. Individuals may compare their lives to the curated, often idealized lives of others, leading to diminished self-esteem and feelings of inadequacy. The constant need to present a perfect image online can create pressure and stress, impacting mental health and well-being[7].

Strategies for Reclaiming Privacy and Genuine Connection

Recognizing the negative impacts of constant connectivity on privacy and personal relationships is the first step towards making positive changes. Here are some strategies to help reclaim privacy and foster genuine connections:

Set Boundaries for Online Sharing

Establish clear boundaries for what you share online. Consider what information is truly necessary to share and what can remain private. Be mindful of the potential consequences of oversharing and prioritize your comfort and privacy[8].

Prioritize In-Person Interactions

Make a conscious effort to prioritize face-to-face interactions over digital communication. Schedule regular meetups with friends and family and engage in activities that allow for meaningful conversations and connections. This can help build deeper, more satisfying relationships[9].

Practice Digital Detoxes

Periodically disconnect from digital devices to recharge and reconnect with the offline world. Digital detoxes can help reduce stress and anxiety, allowing you to focus on meaningful activities and relationships without the constant distraction of technology[10].

Be Authentic

Strive to be authentic in both your online and offline interactions. Share your true self, including both successes and challenges, to foster genuine connections. Authenticity can help create a supportive environment where real emotions and experiences are valued[11].

Seek Professional Help

If the pressure of constant connectivity and the resulting stress and anxiety are overwhelming, consider seeking professional help. Therapy can provide valuable tools and strategies to manage the psychological impacts of constant connectivity and help you reclaim your privacy and well-being[12].

In a world where constant connectivity has become the norm, privacy is increasingly rare. The pressure to share and the resulting superficial interactions can create distance and disconnection in personal relationships. By setting boundaries, prioritizing in-person interactions, and practicing digital detoxes, we can reclaim our privacy and foster genuine connections.

As we navigate the digital age, it is essential to find a balance that allows us to connect meaningfully with others while maintaining our personal boundaries and well-being. Reclaiming privacy and fostering authenticity in our relationships can help bridge the distance created by constant connectivity and lead to more fulfilling and connected lives.

Exercise: Reclaiming Privacy and Building Genuine Connections

This exercise is designed to help you understand and implement the concepts discussed in Chapter 06: "The End of Privacy: How Constant Connectivity Can Create Distance." It aims to encourage self-reflection, create awareness of your privacy boundaries, and develop actionable steps to improve your personal relationships by reclaiming privacy and fostering genuine connections.

Step 1: Self-Reflection

Begin by reflecting on your current online sharing habits and their impact on your sense of privacy and personal relationships. Answer the following questions to gain insight into your behaviors and feelings:

1. Sharing Habits:

- How often do you share personal details online (e.g., on social media, blogs, or forums)?
- What types of information do you usually share (e.g., daily activities, personal milestones, opinions)?

2. Impact on Privacy:

- Do you feel comfortable with the amount of personal information you share online?
- Have you ever experienced regret or discomfort after sharing something online?

3. Impact on Relationships:

- How do your online interactions compare to your face-to-face interactions in terms of depth and meaningfulness?
- Have you noticed any changes in your relationships due to your online presence?

Step 2: Identify Strengths and Weaknesses

Based on your reflections, identify the strengths and weaknesses of your current online sharing habits and their impact on your privacy and relationships:

1. **Strengths:**

    - List three positive aspects of your online sharing habits (e.g., staying connected with distant friends, expressing yourself creatively).
    - Explain how these strengths contribute to your daily life and relationships.

2. **Weaknesses:**

    - List three negative aspects of your online sharing habits (e.g., feeling exposed, experiencing superficial connections).
    - Describe how these weaknesses may be contributing to feelings of discomfort or disconnection.

Step 3: Set Personal Goals for Reclaiming Privacy

Using the insights from your reflections, set two or three specific, achievable goals to reclaim your privacy and enhance your personal relationships. Apply the SMART criteria (Specific, Measurable, Achievable, Relevant, Time-bound) to formulate your goals.

Examples of Goals:

- *"I will limit my social media posts to once a week and focus on sharing meaningful content."*

- *"I will designate one day each week as a 'digital detox' day, where I do not use social media or other digital communication tools."*
- *"I will schedule regular face-to-face meetups with friends and family to strengthen my personal connections."*

Step 4: Develop an Action Plan

To achieve your goals, break them down into smaller, manageable tasks. These tasks should be practical steps you can take to reclaim your privacy and improve your relationships.

1. Goal: Limit Social Media Posts:

- **Task 1:** Review your current social media accounts and privacy settings. Adjust them to limit who can see your posts.
- **Task 2:** Plan your weekly post content to ensure it is meaningful and reflective of your true self.
- **Task 3:** Track your posting habits and any changes in your feelings of privacy and connection in a journal.

2. Goal: Digital Detox Day:

- **Task 1:** Choose a specific day each week for your digital detox.

- **Task 2:** Plan offline activities for your detox day, such as reading, hiking, or spending time with loved ones.
- **Task 3:** Reflect on your digital detox experience and its impact on your well-being and relationships in a journal.

3. **Goal: Schedule Face-to-Face Meetups:**

- **Task 1:** Make a list of friends and family members you want to spend more time with.
- **Task 2**: Reach out to them to schedule regular meetups, such as weekly coffee dates or monthly dinners.
- **Task 3:** Reflect on the quality of your interactions during these meetups and any improvements in your relationships.

Step 5: Monitor and Reflect on Progress

After implementing your action plan, take time to monitor and reflect on your progress:

1. Track Your Progress:

- Keep a journal or use an app to track your completion of tasks and overall progress towards your goals.
- Note any changes in your feelings of privacy, comfort, and relationship satisfaction.

2. Evaluate and Adjust:

- At the end of each week, evaluate the effectiveness of your action plan. Did you meet your goals? What challenges did you encounter?
- Adjust your goals and tasks as needed to better suit your needs and circumstances.

3. Seek Feedback:

- Ask for feedback from friends, family, or a therapist on any noticeable changes in your interactions and relationship quality.
- Use their insights to further refine your approach.

Step 6: Foster Long-Term Changes

To ensure lasting improvements in your privacy and relationship habits, consider the following strategies:

1. Create Lasting Habits:

- Turn successful tasks into long-term habits by integrating them into your daily routine.
- Continuously practice mindfulness and intentional online sharing to maintain a balanced digital life.

2. Stay Accountable:

- Share your goals and progress with a trusted friend or family member who can help keep you accountable.
- Regularly review and adjust your goals to stay on track.

3. Celebrate Progress:

- Celebrate your successes and progress, no matter how small. Acknowledge the positive impact these changes have on your privacy and relationships.

By engaging in this exercise, you can gain a deeper understanding of how constant connectivity impacts your privacy and personal relationships. Taking proactive steps to set boundaries, prioritize face-to-face interactions, and practice digital detoxes can help you reclaim your privacy and foster genuine connections. Remember, the key to enhancing your relationships lies in finding a balance between digital convenience and genuine human connection. Reclaiming privacy and fostering authenticity in your relationships can help bridge the distance created by constant connectivity and lead to more fulfilling and connected lives.

NOTES:

Chapter 07: Echo Chambers and Filter Bubbles: Losing the Human Touch

In the age of digital media, we have unparalleled access to information and the ability to connect with people worldwide. However, the very technologies that offer these opportunities can also create environments that limit our perspectives and deepen social divides. Echo chambers and filter bubbles are terms that describe how digital algorithms and social media can reinforce our existing beliefs and isolate us from differing viewpoints. This chapter explores how these phenomena contribute to loneliness and disconnection, and how we can break free from these confines to regain the human touch in our interactions.

Understanding Echo Chambers and Filter Bubbles

Echo Chambers refer to situations where people are only exposed to opinions and information that reflect and reinforce their own beliefs. This can happen in online communities, social media platforms, and even traditional media outlets, where algorithms and personalized content delivery systems tailor information to our preferences. As a result, our views are echoed back to us, and contrary opinions are filtered out, creating a self-reinforcing cycle[1].

Filter Bubbles are a related concept where algorithms on social media and search engines curate content based on our previous interactions, likes, and shares. This means we are less likely to encounter information that challenges our views. Over time, this creates a bubble around us, filtering out diverse perspectives and isolating us from a broader understanding of the world[2].

The Psychological Impact of Echo Chambers and Filter Bubbles

Confirmation Bias and Narrowed Perspectives

One of the most significant psychological impacts of echo chambers and filter bubbles is the reinforcement of confirmation bias. Confirmation bias is the tendency to seek out, interpret, and remember information that confirms our preexisting beliefs[3]. In a digital environment curated to show us what we want to see, this bias is amplified, making it difficult to engage with or even acknowledge opposing viewpoints. This can lead to a narrowed perspective and a less informed worldview[4].

Social Isolation and Loneliness

Echo chambers and filter bubbles can also contribute to social isolation and loneliness. When our social interactions are limited to people who think like us, we miss out on the richness of diverse opinions and experiences[5]. This can create a false sense of connectedness, where interactions are shallow and do not challenge us to grow or think critically. The lack of meaningful, diverse interactions can lead to feelings of loneliness and isolation, as we are not truly engaging with the full spectrum of human experience[6].

Increased Polarization

The reinforcement of homogeneous beliefs within echo chambers and filter bubbles can contribute to increased polarization. As we become more entrenched in our views, we may become less tolerant of differing opinions and more hostile towards those who hold them[7]. This polarization can strain relationships with family, friends, and colleagues who have different perspectives, further contributing to social fragmentation and loneliness[8].

Breaking Free from Echo Chambers and Filter Bubbles

Recognizing the existence and impact of echo chambers and filter bubbles is the first step towards breaking free from them. Here are some strategies to help broaden your perspectives and foster more meaningful connections:

Diversify Your Information Sources

Actively seek out information from a variety of sources. Read news and opinions from outlets with different political and ideological perspectives. This can help you understand multiple sides of an issue and reduce the effects of confirmation bias. Make a habit of exploring content that challenges your views to develop a more nuanced and informed perspective[9].

Engage in Meaningful Conversations

Seek out conversations with people who have different viewpoints. Approach these discussions with curiosity and an open mind, aiming to understand rather than to persuade. Engaging in respectful dialogue can broaden your horizons and help you build deeper, more meaningful connections[10].

Follow Diverse Voices

On social media, follow accounts and join groups that represent a wide range of perspectives. This can help disrupt the algorithms that create filter bubbles and expose you to a broader array of opinions and experiences. Make a conscious effort to engage with content that challenges your assumptions[11].

Practice Critical Thinking

Developing critical thinking skills can help you navigate the information landscape more effectively. Question the sources of your information, consider the context, and evaluate the evidence presented. This approach can help you identify biases and make more informed decisions about the information you consume[12].

Limit Algorithmic Influence

Take steps to limit the influence of algorithms on your content consumption. This can include using search engines that do not track your browsing history, turning off personalized recommendations on social media, and regularly clearing your browsing data. These actions can help reduce the impact of filter bubbles and expose you to a wider range of content[13].

Reclaiming the Human Touch

Beyond diversifying our information sources and engaging with differing viewpoints, it is essential to reclaim the human touch in our interactions. Here are some ways to foster deeper, more meaningful connections:

Prioritize Face-to-Face Interactions

Make time for in-person interactions with friends, family, and colleagues. Face-to-face conversations allow for richer communication, including non-verbal cues and emotional expressions, which are often lost in digital interactions. These interactions can help build trust and understanding, strengthening your relationships[14].

Cultivate Empathy

Empathy is the ability to understand and share the feelings of others. Cultivating empathy can help bridge divides and foster deeper connections. Practice active listening, put yourself in others' shoes, and be open to experiencing and understanding their emotions and perspectives[15].

Engage in Community Activities

Participating in community activities can help you connect with a diverse group of people and build a sense of belonging. Volunteer, join local clubs or organizations, and attend community events. These activities can provide opportunities to engage with others in meaningful ways and reduce feelings of isolation[16].

Foster Authenticity

Strive to be authentic in your interactions, both online and offline. Share your true self, including your thoughts, feelings, and experiences. Authenticity can create a foundation for genuine connections and help build trust and understanding[17].

Echo chambers and filter bubbles can significantly impact our perspectives and relationships, leading to increased polarization and social isolation. By actively seeking diverse information sources, engaging in meaningful conversations, and fostering empathy and authenticity, we can break free from these confines and regain the human touch in our interactions. As we navigate the digital age, it is essential to balance our online activities with genuine, face-to-face connections that enrich our lives and foster a more inclusive and understanding world. By doing so, we can reduce feelings of loneliness and build stronger, more meaningful relationships.

Exercise: Breaking Free from Echo Chambers and Filter Bubbles

This exercise is designed to help you understand and implement the concepts discussed in Chapter 07: "Echo Chambers and Filter Bubbles: Losing the Human Touch." It aims to encourage self-reflection, broaden your perspectives, and develop actionable steps to foster genuine connections and reduce social isolation.

Step 1: Self-Reflection

Begin by reflecting on your current information consumption habits and their impact on your perspectives and relationships. Answer the following questions to gain insight into your behaviors and feelings:

1. Information Sources:

- What are your primary sources of news and information (e.g., specific websites, social media platforms, news outlets)?
- How often do you engage with information that challenges your views?

2. Social Interactions:

- Do most of your social interactions, both online and offline, involve people who share your viewpoints?
- How do you react when you encounter opinions that differ from your own?

3. Personal Growth:

- Do you feel that your current information consumption habits help you grow and understand the world better?
- Have you noticed any feelings of isolation or polarization in your social interactions?

Step 2: Identify Strengths and Weaknesses

Based on your reflections, identify the strengths and weaknesses of your current information consumption and social interaction habits:

1. Strengths:

- List three positive aspects of your current habits (e.g., staying informed about your interests, feeling supported by like-minded people).
- Explain how these strengths contribute to your daily life and relationships.

2. Weaknesses:

- List three negative aspects of your current habits (e.g., limited exposure to diverse viewpoints, feelings of polarization).
- Describe how these weaknesses may be contributing to feelings of isolation or disconnection.

Step 3: Set Personal Goals for Broadening Perspectives

Using the insights from your reflections, set two or three specific, achievable goals to diversify your information sources and foster more meaningful connections. Apply the **SMART** criteria (**S**pecific, **M**easurable, **A**chievable, **R**elevant, **T**ime-bound) to formulate your goals.

Examples of Goals:

- *"I will read at least one article per week from a news source with a different political or ideological perspective."*
- *"I will engage in a respectful conversation with someone who holds a different viewpoint at least once a month."*
- *"I will join a community group or attend an event that includes people with diverse backgrounds and opinions."*

Step 4: Develop an Action Plan

To achieve your goals, break them down into smaller, manageable tasks. These tasks should be practical steps you can take to broaden your perspectives and improve your relationships.

1. Goal: Read Diverse News Sources:

- **Task 1:** Identify three news sources that represent different political or ideological perspectives from your usual sources.
- **Task 2:** Schedule time each week to read an article from one of these sources.
- **Task 3:** Reflect on the new information and how it compares to your usual sources in a journal.

2. Goal: Engage in Respectful Conversations:

- **Task 1:** Identify friends, family members, or colleagues who hold different viewpoints.
- **Task 2:** Initiate a conversation with them, focusing on listening and understanding their perspective.
- **Task 3:** Reflect on the conversation and what you learned in a journal.

3. **Goal: Join a Community Group:**

   - **Task 1:** Research local community groups, clubs, or events that promote diversity and inclusion.
   - **Task 2:** Attend a meeting or event and actively participate.
   - **Task 3:** Reflect on your experience and any new connections you made in a journal.

Step 5: Monitor and Reflect on Progress

After implementing your action plan, take time to monitor and reflect on your progress:

1. Track Your Progress:

- Keep a journal or use an app to track your completion of tasks and overall progress towards your goals.
- Note any changes in your feelings of connectedness, understanding, and relationship satisfaction.

2. Evaluate and Adjust:

- At the end of each week, evaluate the effectiveness of your action plan. Did you meet your goals? What challenges did you encounter?

- Adjust your goals and tasks as needed to better suit your needs and circumstances.

3. Seek Feedback:

- Ask for feedback from friends, family, or colleagues on any noticeable changes in your interactions and relationship quality.
- Use their insights to further refine your approach.

Step 6: Foster Long-Term Changes

To ensure lasting improvements in your perspectives and relationships, consider the following strategies:

1. Create Lasting Habits:

- Turn successful tasks into long-term habits by integrating them into your daily routine.
- Continuously seek out diverse information sources and engage in meaningful conversations.

2. Stay Accountable:

- Share your goals and progress with a trusted friend or family member who can help keep you accountable.
- Regularly review and adjust your goals to stay on track.

3. Celebrate Progress:

- Celebrate your successes and progress, no matter how small. Acknowledge the positive impact these changes have on your understanding and relationships.

By engaging in this exercise, you can gain a deeper understanding of how echo chambers and filter bubbles impact your perspectives and relationships. Taking proactive steps to diversify your information sources, engage in meaningful conversations, and participate in community activities can help you break free from these confines and foster genuine connections.

Remember, the key to enhancing your relationships and reducing feelings of loneliness lies in finding a balance between digital convenience and genuine human interaction. By doing so, you can build a more inclusive and understanding world, reducing social isolation and fostering stronger, more meaningful relationships.

Chapter 08: Digital Tools for Real Connection: The Positive Side of Tech

In an era often defined by the negative impacts of technology on our social lives, it is easy to overlook the myriad ways in which digital tools can foster genuine human connections. While it is true that technology can sometimes contribute to feelings of loneliness and isolation, it also holds immense potential to bring people together, bridge distances, and create meaningful interactions. This chapter explores the positive side of technology, highlighting how digital tools can enhance our personal relationships and help us build real connections.

Reconnecting with Loved Ones

One of the most significant benefits of digital technology is its ability to reconnect us with friends and family, no matter where they are in the world. Social media platforms, messaging apps, and video calling services have made it easier than ever to stay in touch with loved ones.

Social Media Platforms

Platforms like Facebook, Instagram, and Twitter allow us to keep up with the lives of friends and family members, even if we are miles apart. These platforms enable us to share updates, photos, and videos, helping us feel involved in each other's daily lives. Moreover, social media can facilitate the rekindling of old friendships and the maintenance of relationships that might otherwise fade due to distance and time[1].

Messaging Apps

Apps such as WhatsApp, Telegram, and Signal provide instant, real-time communication. They allow for more private and personalized interactions compared to public social media posts. These apps support not only text but also voice messages, photos, and videos, making communication rich and dynamic[2].

Video Calling Services

Video calling platforms like Zoom, Skype, and FaceTime have revolutionized the way we interact with others. They offer face-to-face communication that can help maintain a sense of closeness and intimacy, even when physical presence is not possible. Regular video calls can help reduce feelings of loneliness and keep relationships strong[3].

Building New Relationships

Technology also opens up avenues for meeting new people and building new relationships. From online communities and forums to dating apps and interest-based groups, digital tools can help us find like-minded individuals and expand our social circles.

Online Communities and Forums

Platforms like Reddit, Quora, and specialized forums cater to a wide array of interests and hobbies. These online communities bring together people with shared passions, enabling them to exchange ideas, support each other, and form friendships. Participating in these communities can provide a sense of belonging and camaraderie[4].

Interest-Based Groups

Apps and websites like Meetup and Eventbrite help people find and join local groups that match their interests. Whether it's a hiking club, a book group, or a coding workshop, these platforms facilitate face-to-face meetings, allowing individuals to connect over shared activities and interests[5].

Dating Apps

Apps like Tinder, Bumble, and OkCupid have transformed the landscape of romantic relationships. These platforms use algorithms to match users based on their preferences and interests, making it easier to find potential partners. While online dating can sometimes lead to superficial interactions, it also offers the possibility of finding meaningful, long-term relationships[6].

Supporting Mental Health

Technology can also play a crucial role in supporting mental health and emotional well-being. Digital tools can provide access to resources, support networks, and professional help, making it easier for individuals to address their mental health needs.

Mental Health Apps

There are numerous apps designed to support mental health, such as Headspace for meditation, Calm for stress relief, and Moodpath for tracking emotional well-being. These apps offer guided exercises, mindfulness techniques, and mood tracking features that can help individuals manage stress and anxiety[7].

Online Therapy

Platforms like BetterHelp and Talkspace provide access to licensed therapists through text, audio, and video sessions. Online therapy offers a convenient and flexible option for those who may find it difficult to attend in-person sessions. It can also reduce the stigma associated with seeking help, making mental health support more accessible[8].

Support Networks

Online support groups and forums can provide a sense of community and understanding for individuals facing similar challenges. Websites like 7 Cups and The Mighty offer peer support and connect users with others who share their experiences. These platforms can help reduce feelings of isolation and provide valuable emotional support[9].

Enhancing Professional Relationships

In the professional realm, technology has transformed the way we network, collaborate, and build relationships. Digital tools can enhance our professional lives by facilitating communication, collaboration, and career growth.

Professional Networking

Platforms like LinkedIn provide opportunities for professional networking and career development. They allow users to connect with colleagues, industry leaders, and potential employers, facilitating knowledge sharing and career advancement. LinkedIn also offers tools for job searching, skill development, and industry news, helping professionals stay informed and connected[10].

Collaboration Tools

Tools like Slack, Microsoft Teams, and Trello have revolutionized workplace communication and collaboration. These platforms enable real-time communication, project management, and file sharing, making it easier for teams to work together, even when they are geographically dispersed. Effective use of these tools can enhance productivity and strengthen professional relationships[11].

Virtual Events and Conferences

The rise of virtual events and conferences has made it possible to connect with industry peers and thought leaders from around the world.

Platforms like Hopin and Zoom support virtual networking, allowing professionals to attend sessions, participate in discussions, and build connections from the comfort of their homes[12].

Bridging Cultural Gaps

Technology also has the potential to bridge cultural gaps and promote understanding and empathy across different communities. Digital tools can facilitate cross-cultural communication and help us appreciate diverse perspectives.

Language Learning Apps

Apps like Duolingo, Babbel, and Rosetta Stone offer accessible and interactive ways to learn new languages. These tools can help break down language barriers and enable more meaningful interactions with people from different cultures[13].

Cultural Exchange Platforms

Websites like Couchsurfing and Workaway connect travelers with local hosts, providing opportunities for cultural exchange and immersion. These platforms allow users to experience different ways of life, fostering understanding and friendship across cultural boundaries[14].

Global Collaboration Projects

Initiatives like Wikipedia and open-source projects bring together contributors from around the world to collaborate on shared goals. These projects demonstrate the power of collective effort and highlight the importance of diverse perspectives in solving global challenges[15].

While technology can sometimes contribute to feelings of loneliness and disconnection, it also holds immense potential to foster genuine human connections. By leveraging digital tools thoughtfully and intentionally, we can enhance our personal relationships, build new connections, support our mental health, and bridge cultural gaps. The key lies in using technology to complement, rather than replace, face-to-face interactions. By embracing the positive aspects of digital tools, we can create a more connected, empathetic, and understanding world.

Exercise: Leveraging Digital Tools for Genuine Connection

This exercise is designed to help you understand and implement the concepts discussed in Chapter 08: "Digital Tools for Real Connection: The Positive Side of Tech." It aims to encourage self-reflection, identify opportunities to use technology positively, and develop actionable steps to enhance your personal and professional relationships.

Step 1: Self-Reflection

Begin by reflecting on your current use of digital tools and their impact on your relationships. Answer the following questions to gain insight into your behaviors and feelings:

1. Current Use of Digital Tools:

- Which digital tools (social media platforms, messaging apps, video calling services, etc.) do you use most frequently?
- How do these tools currently impact your relationships with friends, family, and colleagues?

2. Positive Impacts:

- What are the positive aspects of using these digital tools (e.g., staying connected with distant relatives, meeting new people)?
- How have these tools helped you build or maintain relationships?

3. Areas for Improvement:

- Are there any negative impacts of your current digital tool usage (e.g., feeling overwhelmed, experiencing superficial interactions)?

- In what ways could you use digital tools more effectively to enhance your relationships?

Step 2: Identify Opportunities

Based on your reflections, identify specific opportunities where digital tools can enhance your relationships. Consider both your personal and professional life.

1. Personal Relationships:

- How can you use video calling services to stay connected with loved ones?
- Are there online communities or interest-based groups you could join to meet new people?

2. Professional Relationships:

- How can professional networking platforms help you connect with colleagues and industry leaders?
- Are there collaboration tools that could improve your team's communication and productivity?

Step 3: Set Personal Goals for Using Digital Tools

Using the insights from your reflections, set two or three specific, achievable goals to leverage digital tools for building genuine connections. Apply the **SMART** criteria (**S**pecific, **M**easurable, **A**chievable, **R**elevant, **T**ime-bound) to formulate your goals.

Examples of Goals:

- *"I will schedule a weekly video call with a different family member or friend to stay connected and strengthen our relationships."*
- *"I will join an online community related to one of my hobbies and participate in discussions at least three times a week."*
- *"I will use LinkedIn to reach out to one new professional contact each month and engage in meaningful conversations about our industry."*

Step 4: Develop an Action Plan

To achieve your goals, break them down into smaller, manageable tasks. These tasks should be practical steps you can take to leverage digital tools effectively.

1. **Goal: Schedule Weekly Video Calls:**

   - **Task 1:** Make a list of family members and friends you want to reconnect with.
   - **Task 2:** Send out invitations to schedule weekly video calls.
   - **Task 3:** Prepare conversation topics to ensure meaningful and engaging discussions.

2. **Goal: Join and Participate in an Online Community:**

   - **Task 1:** Research online communities or forums related to your hobbies or interests.
   - **Task 2:** Join the chosen community and introduce yourself.
   - **Task 3:** Participate in discussions by commenting on posts, asking questions, and sharing your experiences.

3. **Goal: Connect with Professional Contacts on LinkedIn:**

   - **Task 1:** Identify professionals in your industry who you would like to connect with.
   - **Task 2:** Send personalized connection requests with a brief introduction and reason for connecting.
   - **Task 3:** Follow up with a message to start a meaningful conversation about industry trends or mutual interests.

Step 5: Monitor and Reflect on Progress

After implementing your action plan, take time to monitor and reflect on your progress:

1. Track Your Progress:

- Keep a journal or use an app to track your completion of tasks and overall progress towards your goals.
- Note any changes in your feelings of connectedness, relationship satisfaction, and professional growth.

2. Evaluate and Adjust:

- At the end of each week, evaluate the effectiveness of your action plan. Did you meet your goals? What challenges did you encounter?
- Adjust your goals and tasks as needed to better suit your needs and circumstances.

3. Seek Feedback:

- Ask for feedback from friends, family, or colleagues on any noticeable changes in your interactions and relationship quality.
- Use their insights to further refine your approach.

Step 6: Foster Long-Term Changes

To ensure lasting improvements in your use of digital tools and relationships, consider the following strategies:

1. **Create Lasting Habits:**

    - Turn successful tasks into long-term habits by integrating them into your daily or weekly routine.
    - Continuously seek out new ways to use digital tools to enhance your relationships.

2. **Stay Accountable:**

    - Share your goals and progress with a trusted friend or family member who can help keep you accountable.
    - Regularly review and adjust your goals to stay on track.

3. **Celebrate Progress:**

    - Celebrate your successes and progress, no matter how small. Acknowledge the positive impact these changes have on your relationships and well-being.

By engaging in this exercise, you can gain a deeper understanding of how digital tools can positively impact your relationships. Taking proactive steps to leverage these tools thoughtfully and intentionally can help you build genuine connections, enhance your personal and professional relationships, and create a more connected, empathetic world.

Remember, the key to using technology effectively lies in finding a balance that complements, rather than replaces, face-to-face interactions. By embracing the positive aspects of digital tools, you can foster stronger, more meaningful connections in your life.

NOTES:

Chapter 09: Fostering Community Online: Success Stories from the Virtual World

In an era where technology has drastically changed the way we interact, the concept of community has taken on new forms. While many lament the loss of traditional, face-to-face communities, there are numerous success stories that highlight how virtual communities can foster deep, meaningful connections and support. This chapter explores how online platforms have created thriving communities, demonstrating the positive impact of technology on human connection.

The Power of Online Communities

Online communities provide spaces where individuals can come together around shared interests, goals, and experiences, regardless of geographical boundaries. These virtual spaces can offer emotional support, knowledge sharing, and a sense of belonging that might be difficult to find in the physical world.

Success Story 1: The Power of Shared Experiences - Reddit's r/AskDocs

Reddit's r/AskDocs is a prime example of how online communities can provide valuable support and information. This subreddit allows users to ask medical questions and receive answers from verified healthcare professionals. The community thrives on the principle of shared knowledge and mutual aid, making medical information more accessible to people around the world.

How It Works

Users post their medical questions, and doctors, nurses, and other healthcare professionals volunteer their time to provide answers and advice. The community is heavily moderated to ensure the accuracy of the information provided and to maintain a respectful and supportive environment[1].

Impact

For many, r/AskDocs serves as a lifeline, offering preliminary medical advice and directing individuals to appropriate care when necessary. It has helped demystify medical conditions, reduce anxiety around health issues, and empower individuals to take proactive steps toward their well-being[2].

Success Story 2: Mental Health Support - 7 Cups

7 Cups is an online platform that connects users with trained listeners and licensed therapists for emotional support. It offers a safe space for individuals to share their struggles and receive empathetic listening and professional guidance.

How It Works

Users can anonymously chat with trained listeners for free or schedule sessions with licensed therapists for a fee. The platform also offers self-help guides, growth paths, and community forums where users can support each other[3].

Impact

7 Cups has become a crucial resource for those dealing with mental health issues, particularly for individuals who may not have access to traditional therapy. It provides immediate emotional support, reduces feelings of isolation, and helps users navigate their mental health challenges with greater resilience[4].

Success Story 3: Professional Networking and Growth – LinkedIn

LinkedIn has revolutionized professional networking, allowing users to build connections, find job opportunities, and engage with industry leaders. It has become an essential tool for career development and professional growth.

How It Works

Users create profiles that highlight their professional experience, skills, and achievements. They can connect with colleagues, join industry-specific groups, and follow companies and influencers to stay informed about trends and opportunities[5].

Impact

LinkedIn has helped millions of professionals advance their careers by providing a platform for networking, knowledge sharing, and personal branding. It fosters a sense of professional community, enabling users to support each other's career journeys and collaborate on projects[6].

Success Story 4: Creative Collaboration – DeviantArt

DeviantArt is an online community for artists to showcase their work, receive feedback, and collaborate on creative projects. It has created a global network of artists who inspire and support each other.

How It Works

Artists can create profiles, upload their artwork, and join groups based on their interests and styles. The platform also offers forums, contests, and commissions, allowing artists to engage with the community and expand their reach[7].

Impact

DeviantArt has been instrumental in helping artists gain exposure, improve their skills, and find opportunities for collaboration. It has fostered a supportive environment where creativity thrives, and artists can connect with like-minded individuals from around the world[8].

Success Story 5: Learning and Education - Khan Academy

Khan Academy is a non-profit educational organization that provides free online courses and resources for students of all ages. It has democratized education, making high-quality learning accessible to anyone with an internet connection.

How It Works

Khan Academy offers a wide range of subjects, from math and science to humanities and computer programming. Users can watch video lessons, complete practice exercises, and track their progress. The platform also provides tools for teachers and parents to support their students' learning[9].

Impact

Khan Academy has empowered millions of learners worldwide to pursue their educational goals. It has bridged educational gaps, provided supplemental learning for students, and offered professional development opportunities for educators. The platform exemplifies how technology can enhance education and foster a global learning community[10].

Success Story 6: Social Activism and Support - Change.org

Change.org is a petition platform that enables people to start and support campaigns for social, political, and environmental causes. It has become a powerful tool for grassroots activism and collective action.

How It Works

Users can create petitions on various issues and share them through social media and email. Supporters can sign petitions, leave comments, and share the campaigns with their networks to garner more support[11].

Impact

Change.org has empowered individuals to drive change on important issues, from local community concerns to global movements. Successful campaigns have led to policy changes, raised awareness, and mobilized communities to take action. The platform demonstrates the potential of technology to amplify voices and create real-world impact[12].

Strategies for Building Successful Online Communities

The success of these virtual communities can be attributed to several key factors:

1. Shared Purpose: Successful online communities are built around a common interest or goal that unites members and fosters a sense of belonging[13].

2. Accessibility: These platforms make it easy for users to join, participate, and contribute, regardless of their location or background[14].

3. Supportive Environment: A positive and respectful atmosphere encourages engagement and helps build trust among members[15].

4. Moderation and Governance: Effective moderation and clear guidelines ensure that the community remains safe, welcoming, and focused on its purpose[16].

5. Diverse Participation: Encouraging a wide range of perspectives and experiences enriches the community and promotes learning and growth[17].

While technology can sometimes create barriers to human connection, it also offers incredible opportunities to build and sustain meaningful communities. The success stories of Reddit's r/AskDocs, 7 Cups, LinkedIn, DeviantArt, Khan Academy, and Change.org highlight how online platforms can foster deep connections, provide support, and drive positive change. By understanding the principles that make these communities thrive, we can harness the power of technology to create our own supportive and impactful virtual spaces. As we navigate the digital age, let us celebrate and contribute to the communities that bring us together, enrich our lives, and help us achieve our collective goals.

Exercise: Building and Engaging with Online Communities

This exercise is designed to help you understand and implement the concepts discussed in Chapter 09: "Fostering Community Online: Success Stories from the Virtual World." It aims to encourage self-reflection, identify opportunities to engage with online communities, and develop actionable steps to create or participate in meaningful virtual spaces.

Step 1: Self-Reflection
Begin by reflecting on your current engagement with online communities and their impact on your sense of connection and support. Answer the following questions to gain insight into your behaviors and feelings:

1. Current Engagement:

- Which online communities are you currently a part of (e.g., forums, social media groups, professional networks)?
- How often do you engage with these communities, and in what ways (e.g., posting, commenting, lurking)?

2. Positive Impacts:

- What benefits have you experienced from participating in these communities (e.g., support, knowledge, friendship)?
- How have these communities helped you feel connected and supported?

3. Areas for Improvement:

- Are there any challenges or drawbacks you've encountered in these communities (e.g., negativity, lack of engagement)?
- In what ways could you increase your participation or improve your experience in these communities?

Step 2: Identify Opportunities

Based on your reflections, identify specific opportunities where you can engage more meaningfully with online communities or create your own. Consider both personal and professional contexts.

1. Personal Communities:

- Are there interest-based groups or forums you've been wanting to join (e.g., hobby groups, support communities)?
- How can you contribute to these communities in a way that adds value and fosters connection?

2. Professional Communities:

- Are there professional networks or industry-specific groups that could benefit your career development?
- How can you leverage these communities to build relationships, share knowledge, and advance your career?

Step 3: Set Personal Goals for Online Community Engagement

Using the insights from your reflections, set two or three specific, achievable goals to engage more meaningfully with online communities. Apply the SMART criteria (Specific, Measurable, Achievable, Relevant, Time-bound) to formulate your goals.

Examples of Goals:

- *"I will join an online community related to my favorite hobby and participate in discussions at least twice a week."*
- *"I will connect with five new professionals in my industry on LinkedIn and engage with their posts and articles regularly."*
- *"I will create a support group for individuals with similar experiences and host monthly virtual meetups."*

Step 4: Develop an Action Plan

To achieve your goals, break them down into smaller, manageable tasks. These tasks should be practical steps you can take to engage with or create online communities effectively.

1. **Goal: Join and Participate in an Online Hobby Community:**

   - **Task 1:** Research online communities or forums related to your hobby.
   - **Task 2:** Join the chosen community and introduce yourself.
   - **Task 3:** Participate in discussions by commenting on posts, sharing your own experiences, and asking questions.

2. **Goal: Connect with Professionals on LinkedIn:**

   - **Task 1:** Identify professionals in your industry who you would like to connect with.
   - **Task 2:** Send personalized connection requests with a brief introduction and reason for connecting.
   - **Task 3:** Engage with their posts by liking, commenting, and sharing valuable insights.

3. **Goal: Create a Support Group and Host Virtual Meetups:**

   - **Task 1:** Identify a platform for hosting your support group (e.g., Facebook Groups, Zoom).
   - **Task 2:** Create the group and invite individuals with similar experiences.

- **Task 3:** Plan and host monthly virtual meetups, preparing discussion topics and activities in advance.

Step 5: Monitor and Reflect on Progress

After implementing your action plan, take time to monitor and reflect on your progress:

1. Track Your Progress:

- Keep a journal or use an app to track your completion of tasks and overall progress towards your goals.
- Note any changes in your feelings of connectedness, support, and relationship satisfaction.

2. Evaluate and Adjust:

- At the end of each week, evaluate the effectiveness of your action plan. Did you meet your goals? What challenges did you encounter?
- Adjust your goals and tasks as needed to better suit your needs and circumstances.

3. Seek Feedback:

- Ask for feedback from friends, community members, or colleagues on any noticeable changes in your interactions and relationship quality.
- Use their insights to further refine your approach.

Step 6: Foster Long-Term Changes

To ensure lasting improvements in your online community engagement and relationships, consider the following strategies:

1. Create Lasting Habits:

- Turn successful tasks into long-term habits by integrating them into your daily or weekly routine.
- Continuously seek out new ways to contribute and add value to your communities.

2. Stay Accountable:

- Share your goals and progress with a trusted friend or community member who can help keep you accountable.
- Regularly review and adjust your goals to stay on track.

3. Celebrate Progress:

- Celebrate your successes and progress, no matter how small. Acknowledge the positive impact these changes have on your sense of community and well-being.

By engaging in this exercise, you can gain a deeper understanding of how to leverage online communities to enhance your sense of connection and support. Taking proactive steps to participate in or create meaningful virtual spaces can help you build genuine relationships, find support, and achieve your personal and professional goals. Remember, the key to successful online community engagement lies in active participation, mutual support, and continuous learning. By embracing the positive aspects of digital communities, you can foster a more connected, supportive, and fulfilling virtual world.

Chapter 10: The Future of Interaction: Innovations Bringing Us Closer

As we navigate an increasingly digital world, technology continues to evolve, shaping the way we interact with one another. Despite concerns about technology contributing to loneliness and isolation, numerous innovations are emerging that aim to bring us closer together. This chapter explores the future of interaction, highlighting groundbreaking technologies that have the potential to foster deeper connections, enhance communication, and bridge distances.

Virtual Reality (VR) and Augmented Reality (AR)

Virtual Reality (VR) and Augmented Reality (AR) are at the forefront of immersive technology, transforming the way we experience and interact with the digital world. These technologies offer new ways to connect with others, providing opportunities for more engaging and meaningful interactions.

Virtual Reality (VR)

VR creates fully immersive, three-dimensional environments that users can explore and interact with using specialized headsets and controllers. This technology has the potential to revolutionize social interactions by creating shared virtual spaces where people can meet, collaborate, and engage in activities together, regardless of physical location.

Applications in Social Interaction:

- **Virtual Meetups:** Platforms like VRChat and AltspaceVR allow users to create avatars and meet in virtual spaces, fostering a sense of presence and togetherness that transcends geographical barriers[1].

- **Virtual Workspaces:** VR is being used to create virtual offices where remote teams can collaborate in real-time, enhancing the sense of camaraderie and teamwork[2].

- **Social Events:** From virtual concerts to online gaming, VR provides unique opportunities for shared experiences that feel remarkably real and engaging[3].

Augmented Reality (AR)

AR overlays digital information onto the physical world, enhancing our real-world interactions with virtual elements. By integrating digital content into our everyday environments, AR can create new ways to connect and communicate.

Applications in Social Interaction:

- **Enhanced Communication:** AR can be used in video calls to display real-time data, interactive elements, and contextual information, making conversations more dynamic and informative[4].

- **Shared Experiences:** Apps like Pokémon Go and other AR games encourage users to explore their surroundings and interact with others, blending the virtual and physical worlds in engaging ways[5].

- **Education and Training:** AR can facilitate collaborative learning and training by providing interactive, hands-on experiences that can be shared with others[6].

Artificial Intelligence (AI) and Machine Learning

Artificial Intelligence (AI) and Machine Learning are transforming communication by making it more personalized, efficient, and responsive. These technologies can enhance our interactions, making them more meaningful and impactful.

AI-Powered Communication Tools

AI is being integrated into various communication platforms to improve the quality and effectiveness of our interactions. These tools can help bridge language barriers, provide real-time assistance, and personalize our communication experiences.

Applications in Social Interaction:

- **Real-Time Translation:** Tools like Google Translate and Microsoft Translator use AI to provide real-time translation, enabling seamless communication between people who speak different languages[7].

- **Virtual Assistants:** AI-powered virtual assistants like Siri, Alexa, and Google Assistant can help manage schedules, set reminders, and facilitate communication, making it easier to stay connected with others[8].

- **Personalized Content:** AI algorithms can curate content tailored to our interests and preferences, helping us discover new connections and engage with relevant communities[9].

AI in Mental Health Support

AI is also playing a significant role in mental health support, providing accessible and personalized assistance to those in need. These innovations can help reduce feelings of isolation and provide critical support.

Applications in Mental Health:

- **Chatbots and Virtual Therapists:** AI-powered chatbots like Woebot and virtual therapists like Wysa offer real-time mental health support, providing users with coping strategies, emotional support, and resources[10].

- **Predictive Analytics:** AI can analyze patterns in behavior and communication to identify signs of mental health issues, enabling early intervention and support[11].

The Internet of Things (IoT)

The Internet of Things (IoT) refers to the network of interconnected devices that communicate and exchange data. This technology is enhancing our ability to connect and interact with our environment and each other in meaningful ways.

Smart Home Devices

IoT-enabled smart home devices are making our living spaces more interactive and connected, fostering a sense of community and support.

Applications in Social Interaction:

- **Smart Assistants:** Devices like Amazon Echo and Google Home can facilitate communication by making it easy to connect with family and friends through voice commands[12].

- **Health Monitoring:** Wearable devices like Fitbit and Apple Watch track health metrics and can share this data with loved ones or healthcare providers, promoting well-being and connectedness[13].

Community Engagement

IoT is also enhancing community engagement by providing tools that connect people and foster collaboration.

Applications in Community Building:

- **Smart Cities**: IoT technologies are being used to create smart cities that enhance community living through connected infrastructure, improving communication, transportation, and public services[14].

- **Local Networks:** IoT can enable the creation of hyper-local networks that connect neighbors, facilitate resource sharing, and promote community activities[15].

Blockchain Technology

Blockchain technology, known for its use in cryptocurrencies, is also being explored for its potential to enhance trust and transparency in social interactions.

Decentralized Social Networks

Blockchain can be used to create decentralized social networks that prioritize user privacy and control over personal data, fostering more authentic and secure interactions.

Applications in Social Interaction:

- **Privacy and Security:** Blockchain ensures that users have control over their data, enhancing privacy and security in online interactions[16].

- **Trust and Authenticity:** Decentralized networks can reduce the spread of misinformation and increase trust in online communities by providing transparent and verifiable records of interactions[17].

As technology continues to evolve, it brings with it the potential to transform our interactions and bring us closer together. Innovations in VR, AR, AI, IoT, and blockchain are creating new opportunities for meaningful connections, enhancing communication, and fostering a sense of community. By embracing these technologies thoughtfully and intentionally, we can harness their power to build a more connected and supportive world.

The future of interaction is not just about overcoming the challenges of loneliness and isolation but about creating a digital landscape that enhances our humanity and strengthens our bonds with one another.

As we look to the future, let us celebrate and leverage these innovations to bring us closer, fostering a sense of belonging and connection in an increasingly digital world.

Exercise: Embracing Future Technologies for Deeper Connections

This exercise is designed to help you understand and implement the concepts discussed in Chapter 10: "The Future of Interaction: Innovations Bringing Us Closer." It aims to encourage exploration of emerging technologies, identify opportunities to enhance personal and professional interactions, and develop actionable steps to leverage these innovations for deeper connections.

Step 1: Self-Assessment

Begin by assessing your current use of technology and its impact on your interactions. Answer the following questions to gain insight into your behaviors and identify areas for improvement:

1. Current Technology Use:

- What types of technology do you currently use to interact with others (e.g., social media, video calls, messaging apps)?

- How often do you use these technologies for personal and professional interactions?

2. Impact on Relationships:

- How has technology positively impacted your relationships (e.g., staying connected with distant relatives, collaborating with remote colleagues)?
- Are there any negative impacts you've noticed (e.g., feeling disconnected despite frequent communication, over-reliance on digital interactions)?

3. Opportunities for Improvement:

- What new technologies are you interested in exploring (e.g., VR, AR, AI-powered tools)?
- How do you think these technologies could enhance your interactions and relationships?

Step 2: Set Personal Goals

Using the insights from your self-assessment, set two or three specific, achievable goals to explore and integrate new technologies into your interactions. Apply the **SMART** criteria (**S**pecific, **M**easurable, **A**chievable, **R**elevant, **T**ime-bound) to formulate your goals.

Examples of Goals:

- "I will participate in a VR social event once a month to explore virtual meetups and enhance my social interactions."
- "I will use an AI-powered mental health app daily for the next three months to support my emotional well-being and reduce feelings of isolation."
- "I will join a local IoT community network and attend their events to engage more with my neighborhood and build local connections."

Step 3: Develop an Action Plan

To achieve your goals, break them down into smaller, manageable tasks. These tasks should be practical steps you can take to explore and integrate new technologies effectively.

1. Goal: Participate in a VR Social Event:

- **Task 1:** Research VR platforms that host social events (e.g., VRChat, AltspaceVR).
- **Task 2:** Create an account and set up your VR equipment.
- **Task 3:** Browse and sign up for a social event that interests you.

- **Task 4:** Attend the event and engage with other participants.

2. Goal: Use an AI-Powered Mental Health App:

- **Task 1:** Research and choose an AI-powered mental health app (e.g., Woebot, Wysa).
- **Task 2:** Download and install the app on your device.
- **Task 3:** Set daily reminders to use the app and engage with its features.
- **Task 4:** Track your mood and progress over the next three months.

3. Goal: Join a Local IoT Community Network:

- **Task 1:** Research local IoT community networks or smart city initiatives in your area.
- **Task 2:** Join the community network and introduce yourself.
- **Task 3:** Attend their events or meetings regularly.
- **Task 4:** Participate in discussions and collaborate on community projects.

Step 4: Monitor and Reflect on Progress

After implementing your action plan, take time to monitor and reflect on your progress:

1. Track Your Progress:

- Keep a journal or use an app to track your completion of tasks and overall progress towards your goals.
- Note any changes in your feelings of connectedness, relationship satisfaction, and technology engagement.

2. Evaluate and Adjust:

- At the end of each month, evaluate the effectiveness of your action plan. Did you meet your goals? What challenges did you encounter?
- Adjust your goals and tasks as needed to better suit your needs and circumstances.

3. Seek Feedback:

- Ask for feedback from friends, family, or colleagues on any noticeable changes in your interactions and relationship quality.
- Use their insights to further refine your approach.

Step 5: Foster Long-Term Changes

To ensure lasting improvements in your use of technology and relationships, consider the following strategies:

1. **Create Lasting Habits:**

   - Turn successful tasks into long-term habits by integrating them into your daily or weekly routine.
   - Continuously seek out new ways to use emerging technologies to enhance your interactions.

2. **Stay Accountable:**

   - Share your goals and progress with a trusted friend or family member who can help keep you accountable.
   - Regularly review and adjust your goals to stay on track.

3. **Celebrate Progress:**

   - Celebrate your successes and progress, no matter how small. Acknowledge the positive impact these changes have on your sense of connection and well-being.

By engaging in this exercise, you can gain a deeper understanding of how to leverage emerging technologies to enhance your interactions and relationships. Taking proactive steps to explore and integrate new digital tools can help you build genuine connections, reduce feelings of isolation, and create a more connected and supportive world.

Remember, the key to successful technology use lies in thoughtful and intentional engagement. By embracing the positive aspects of innovations like VR, AR, AI, IoT, and blockchain, you can foster stronger, more meaningful connections in your life.

NOTES:

Chapter 11: The Art of Mindful Technology Use: Creating Healthy Digital Habits

In an era where technology is deeply woven into the fabric of our daily lives, learning to use it mindfully can be transformative. Mindful technology use is not about eschewing digital devices altogether but about creating a balanced relationship with them. By cultivating healthy digital habits, we can harness technology to enhance our lives while minimizing its potential to contribute to feelings of loneliness and disconnection.

Understanding Mindful Technology Use

Mindfulness is the practice of being present and fully engaged with whatever we're doing at the moment. When applied to technology, mindfulness involves being aware of our interactions with digital devices and intentionally choosing how, when, and why we use them. This approach contrasts sharply with the habitual and often unconscious use of technology that many of us have fallen into[1].

The Impact of Unmindful Technology Use

Unmindful technology use can lead to several negative outcomes, including increased stress, reduced productivity, and strained relationships. For instance, the constant barrage of notifications can create a sense of urgency and distraction, pulling us away from the present moment and the people around us. Prolonged screen time, especially on social media, can exacerbate feelings of inadequacy and loneliness as we compare our lives to the curated highlights of others[2].

Steps to Cultivate Mindful Technology Use

1. Set Intentions for Technology Use

Begin by setting clear intentions for how you want to use technology. Ask yourself what you hope to achieve and how you want to feel after your digital interactions. Whether it's staying connected with loved ones, learning new skills, or simply enjoying entertainment, having a clear purpose can help you use technology more mindfully[3].

2. Create Boundaries and Limits

Establish boundaries for when and where you use digital devices. Designate tech-free zones and times, such as during meals, before bed, or while spending quality time with family and friends. These boundaries help create a healthier balance between digital and real-world interactions[4].

3. Practice Digital Detoxes

Regularly schedule periods where you completely disconnect from technology. A digital detox can be as short as an hour or as long as a weekend. Use this time to engage in offline activities that bring you joy and fulfillment, such as reading, exercising, or spending time in nature[5].

4. Be Selective with Content Consumption

Be mindful of the content you consume and how it makes you feel. Curate your digital environment by unfollowing accounts that contribute to negative emotions and following those that inspire and uplift you. Additionally, limit your exposure to news and social media, which can often be sources of stress and anxiety[6].

5. Engage in Single-Tasking

Multitasking with technology, such as checking emails during meetings or scrolling through social media while watching TV, can lead to decreased productivity and increased stress. Practice single-tasking by focusing on one digital task at a time and giving it your full attention[7].

Tools and Strategies for Mindful Technology Use

1. Use Technology to Manage Technology

Leverage apps and settings that promote mindful use. Many smartphones offer features like screen time tracking, app usage limits, and do-not-disturb modes. These tools can help you monitor and manage your digital habits more effectively[8].

2. Adopt the Pomodoro Technique

The Pomodoro Technique, which involves working in focused intervals followed by short breaks, can be applied to digital tasks. This method encourages concentrated work periods, reducing the temptation to switch between tasks or engage in mindless browsing[9].

3. Mindful Breathing and Meditation Apps

Incorporate mindfulness practices into your routine with the help of apps designed for meditation and mindful breathing. These apps can provide guided sessions that help you stay grounded and present, even amidst a busy digital schedule[10].

4. Reflect and Adjust Regularly

Periodically reflect on your technology use and its impact on your well-being. Consider keeping a journal to track your digital habits and their effects on your mood and productivity. Use these reflections to make adjustments and set new goals for mindful technology use[11].

The Benefits of Mindful Technology Use

By adopting mindful technology practices, you can experience a range of benefits that enhance both your digital and real-world experiences.

1. Improved Mental Health

Mindful technology use can reduce feelings of anxiety, stress, and loneliness. By being intentional about your digital interactions, you create space for activities that promote mental well-being, such as exercise, hobbies, and socializing in person[12].

2. Enhanced Relationships

Setting boundaries for technology use allows you to be more present in your relationships. By minimizing distractions, you can engage in deeper, more meaningful conversations and strengthen your connections with loved ones[13].

3. Increased Productivity and Focus

When you use technology mindfully, you are better able to focus on important tasks and avoid the pitfalls of multitasking. This leads to greater productivity and a sense of accomplishment[14].

4. Greater Life Satisfaction

Mindful technology use helps you align your digital habits with your values and goals. By being intentional about how you spend your time online, you can create a more fulfilling and balanced life[15].

In a world where technology is omnipresent, learning to use it mindfully is essential for maintaining our well-being. By setting intentions, creating boundaries, and using digital tools thoughtfully, we can cultivate healthy digital habits that enhance our lives rather than detract from them. The art of mindful technology use is not about rejecting digital devices but about embracing them in a way that promotes connection, balance, and overall happiness. As we navigate the digital landscape with greater awareness, we can transform our relationship with technology and lead more fulfilling lives.

Results-Oriented Exercise: Mindful Technology Use Plan
To help you implement the concepts discussed in this chapter, follow this step-by-step exercise designed to create your own Mindful Technology Use Plan. This exercise will guide you through setting intentions, establishing boundaries, and integrating mindful practices into your digital life.

Step 1: Set Your Intentions

1. Reflect on Your Current Technology Use
- Spend 10 minutes reflecting on how you currently use technology. Write down your thoughts in a journal. Consider questions like:
  ✓ How much time do I spend on my phone/computer each day?
  ✓ What apps or websites do I use the most?
  ✓ How do I feel after using technology?

2. Define Your Goals

- Write down 3-5 specific goals for your technology use. Examples:
  ✓ Reduce daily screen time by 1 hour.
  ✓ Use social media only for connecting with friends and family.
  ✓ Limit news consumption to 30 minutes per day.

Step 2: Establish Boundaries

1. Identify Tech-Free Zones and Times

- Choose specific areas and times in your life where you will not use technology.
  Examples:
- ✓ No phones during meals.
- ✓ No screen time 1 hour before bed.
- ✓ Tech-free weekends or evenings.

2. Create a Schedule

- ✓ Develop a daily or weekly schedule that includes designated times for technology use and tech-free periods. Write it down and place it somewhere visible.

Step 3: Practice Digital Detoxes

1. Plan a Digital Detox

- ✓ Choose a day or weekend for a digital detox. Inform friends and family so they are aware of your plans. Prepare activities to engage in during your detox, such as reading, hiking, or spending time with loved ones.

2. Reflect on Your Detox Experience

- ✓ After completing your digital detox, spend 10-15 minutes reflecting on the experience.
  Write down your thoughts:

- ✓ How did you feel without technology?
- ✓ What activities did you enjoy the most?
- ✓ What did you learn about your relationship with technology?

Step 4: Be Selective with Content Consumption

1. Audit Your Digital Environment

- ✓ Spend 30 minutes reviewing the apps, websites, and social media accounts you follow. Unfollow or delete any that do not align with your goals or that contribute to negative feelings.

2. Curate Positive Content

- ✓ Identify and follow accounts or subscribe to content that inspires and uplifts you. Make a list of 5-10 positive sources you want to engage with regularly.

Step 5: Engage in Single-Tasking

1. Practice Single-Tasking Daily

- ✓ Choose one daily activity where you will practice single-tasking.

  Examples:
- ✓ Checking and responding to emails without multitasking.
- ✓ Watching a video or reading an article without distractions.
- ✓ Set a timer for 25 minutes (using the Pomodoro Technique) and focus solely on the chosen task.

2. Reflect on Single-Tasking Sessions

- At the end of each week, spend 10 minutes reflecting on your single-tasking sessions.

  Write down:
- ✓ How did focusing on one task at a time affect your productivity?
- ✓ How did you feel compared to when you multitask?

Step 6: Utilize Mindfulness Tools and Apps

1. Download and Explore Mindfulness Apps

- Choose a mindfulness app (e.g., Headspace, Calm) and explore its features. Try a guided meditation or breathing exercise.

2. Incorporate Mindfulness Practices into Your Routine

- Schedule a 5-10 minute mindfulness session each day using the app. Focus on being present and aware during these sessions.

Step 7: Regular Reflection and Adjustment

1. Keep a Technology Use Journal

- Dedicate a journal to tracking your technology use and mindfulness practices. Write daily or weekly entries about your experiences, challenges, and progress.

2. Adjust Your Plan as Needed

- At the end of each month, review your journal and assess your progress toward your goals. Make any necessary adjustments to your Mindful Technology Use Plan to better align with your intentions and lifestyle.

By following this exercise, you will develop a personalized approach to mindful technology use, enhancing your well-being and fostering a healthier relationship with your digital devices.

Chapter 12: From Online to Offline: Translating Digital Connections into Real-World Relationships

In our hyper-connected digital age, forming connections online has become second nature. Social media platforms, online communities, and messaging apps make it easier than ever to meet and communicate with people from all walks of life. Despite this unprecedented level of connectivity, many still feel a profound sense of loneliness. The challenge lies in translating these digital connections into meaningful real-world relationships. In this chapter, we explore how to bridge the gap between our online interactions and offline lives, creating deeper, more fulfilling connections.

The Digital Connection Paradox

Digital platforms offer a paradox of connection and isolation. While they enable us to stay in touch with friends and meet new people, the interactions can often be superficial. Likes, comments, and shares, though seemingly engaging, lack the depth and nuance of face-to-face communication. This superficiality can lead to a sense of emptiness and longing for more meaningful interactions[1].

The first step in bridging this gap is recognizing the limitations of online interactions. Understanding that digital connections are merely a starting point, not an endpoint, is crucial. Our goal should be to use these platforms as tools to initiate relationships that can be nurtured and developed offline[2].

Building a Foundation for Real-World Relationships

1. Authenticity Online

Authenticity is the cornerstone of any meaningful relationship, whether online or offline. Presenting an honest and genuine version of yourself online sets the stage for authentic connections. Avoid the temptation to curate a perfect image. Instead, share your real thoughts, feelings, and experiences. This vulnerability fosters trust and invites others to do the same[3].

2. Active Engagement

Passive consumption of content is a common pitfall of social media use. To build real connections, shift from passive scrolling to active engagement. Comment thoughtfully on posts, initiate conversations, and reach out to people who share your interests.

Genuine engagement shows that you value the connection and are interested in fostering a deeper relationship[4].

3. Identify Common Interests

Shared interests are a natural bridge between online and offline interactions. Join online communities or groups centered around your hobbies and passions. Participate actively and look for opportunities to connect with members outside the digital space. Whether it's a book club, fitness group, or professional network, common interests can serve as a foundation for real-world relationships[5].

Transitioning from Online to Offline

1. Initiate Offline Meetings

Once you've established a connection online, take the initiative to suggest meeting in person. Start with casual, low-pressure environments such as coffee shops or public events. Express your interest in getting to know the person better and suggest a specific time and place to meet. Clear communication and genuine interest are key to a successful transition[6].

2. Leverage Shared Activities

Suggesting activities that you both enjoy can make the transition smoother. If you've bonded over a shared love for hiking, propose a weekend hike. If you're both food enthusiasts, plan to visit a new restaurant together. Shared activities provide a comfortable and engaging way to deepen your relationship beyond the screen[7].

3. Attend Group Events

If meeting one-on-one feels intimidating, consider attending group events together. This can be a social gathering, a community event, or a meetup organized around your common interest. Group settings can alleviate the pressure of one-on-one interactions and offer a more relaxed environment to connect[8].

Cultivating Real-World Relationships

1. Prioritize Quality Time

Once you've started meeting offline, prioritize quality time together. Make an effort to see each other regularly and engage in meaningful conversations. Quality time strengthens bonds and helps build a solid foundation for your relationship[9].

2. Be Present

In our technology-driven world, being fully present during face-to-face interactions is increasingly rare but immensely valuable. Put away your phone, maintain eye contact, and actively listen to the other person. Being present demonstrates respect and genuine interest, fostering a deeper connection[10].

3. Communicate Openly

Open and honest communication is vital in any relationship. Share your thoughts, feelings, and experiences, and encourage the other person to do the same. Address any misunderstandings or issues promptly and constructively. Healthy communication builds trust and strengthens your bond[11].

Nurturing Long-Distance Relationships

Not all online connections can transition to regular in-person meetings, especially if distance is a factor. However, long-distance relationships can still be meaningful and fulfilling with intentional effort.

1. Regular Communication

Consistent and meaningful communication is the lifeblood of long-distance relationships. Schedule regular calls or video chats and make an effort to stay updated on each other's lives. Sharing everyday moments, even from afar, helps maintain a sense of closeness[12].

2. Plan Visits

Whenever possible, plan visits to spend quality time together. Having something to look forward to can strengthen your bond and provide motivation to maintain the relationship. Make the most of these visits by creating lasting memories together[13].

3. Be Supportive

Support is crucial in any relationship, but it's even more important in long-distance ones. Celebrate each other's achievements, offer encouragement during tough times, and be a reliable source of support. Emotional availability bridges the physical distance and fosters a deep connection[14].

The Role of Technology in Sustaining Real-World Relationships

While the goal is to translate digital connections into real-world relationships, technology can still play a supportive role in maintaining these relationships. Here's how:

1. Stay Connected with Messaging Apps

Use messaging apps to stay in touch between in-person meetings. Share updates, send thoughtful messages, and keep the communication flowing. These small gestures can reinforce your connection and show that you care[15].

2. Share Experiences Virtually

When you can't be together physically, share experiences virtually. Watch a movie together using streaming services, play online games, or cook the same recipe and enjoy a virtual meal. These shared activities can create a sense of togetherness despite the physical distance[16].

3. Use Social Media Wisely

Use social media to complement your real-world interactions, not replace them. Share moments from your life, but also make an effort to interact meaningfully with the other person's posts. A balanced approach to social media use can help maintain your connection without becoming a distraction[17].

Translating digital connections into real-world relationships requires intentional effort, authenticity, and a willingness to step outside our comfort zones. By prioritizing quality interactions, being present, and leveraging technology thoughtfully, we can bridge the gap between our online and offline worlds. These meaningful relationships enrich our lives, providing the connection and fulfillment that digital interactions alone cannot offer. As we navigate the complexities of modern communication, let's remember that the most profound connections are those that extend beyond the screen and into our everyday lives.

Exercise: Translating Digital Connections into Real-World Relationships

This exercise is designed to help you take practical steps to translate your digital connections into meaningful real-world relationships. Follow the steps below to apply the concepts from this chapter and enhance your understanding and implementation of these ideas.

Step 1: Assess Your Current Digital Connections

1. List Your Digital Connections

- Write down a list of people you frequently interact with online. Include friends, acquaintances, and members of online communities you are part of.

2. Evaluate the Depth of Each Connection

- For each person on your list, rate the depth of your relationship on a scale from 1 to 5 (1 being superficial, 5 being very deep). Reflect on why you rated them as you did.

Step 2: Identify Potential for Real-World Relationships

1. Select Candidates for Offline Interaction

- Choose 3-5 people from your list who you would like to build deeper, real-world relationships with. Consider those with shared interests or common values.

2. Set Goals for Each Connection

- Write down specific goals for transitioning each selected digital connection to an offline relationship. Example goals could be meeting for coffee, attending an event together, or planning a group outing.

Step 3: Take Action to Initiate Offline Meetings

1. Reach Out with a Personal Message

- Send a personal message to each person you selected, expressing your interest in meeting up offline. Be genuine and suggest specific dates, times, and activities.

2. Plan a Meet-Up

- Organize a meet-up with at least one person from your list. Choose a comfortable setting for both parties, such as a coffee shop, park, or public event.

Step 4: Engage in Meaningful Offline Activities

1. Participate in Shared Activities

- Plan an activity based on a shared interest. This could be attending a local event, participating in a hobby together, or exploring a new place.

2. Be Present and Authentic

- During your meet-up, practice being fully present. Put away your phone, maintain eye contact, and actively listen to the other person. Share your genuine thoughts and experiences to foster a deeper connection.

Step 5: Reflect and Adjust

1. Reflect on Your Experience

- After each meet-up, spend 10-15 minutes reflecting on the experience. Write down what went well, what could be improved, and how the interaction made you feel.

2. Adjust Your Approach

- Based on your reflections, adjust your approach for future meet-ups. Consider what activities were most enjoyable, how you can be more present, and any new goals you want to set for your relationships.

Step 6: Nurture Long-Distance Relationships

1. Schedule Regular Communication

- For long-distance connections, set a regular schedule for video calls or phone chats. Consistent communication helps maintain the relationship despite the distance.

2. Plan Visits When Possible

- Plan occasional visits to spend quality time together. Use these opportunities to create lasting memories and strengthen your bond.

Step 7: Use Technology to Support Real-World Relationships

1. Stay Connected Through Messaging Apps

- Use messaging apps to share updates, send thoughtful messages, and keep the communication flowing between in-person meetings.

2. Share Virtual Experiences

- When you can't be together physically, share experiences virtually. Watch a movie together online, play an online game, or cook the same meal and enjoy a virtual dinner.

By following these steps, you will be able to translate your digital connections into meaningful real-world relationships, enriching your life and the lives of those you connect with. This exercise will help you put the concepts from this chapter into practice, leading to deeper and more fulfilling connections.

NOTES:

Chapter 13: Designing for Togetherness: How Developers Can Enhance Human Connection

In an age dominated by digital interactions, the role of technology developers has never been more crucial. While technology has the potential to isolate us, it also holds immense power to bring us together. By intentionally designing digital products and platforms with human connection in mind, developers can foster a sense of community and togetherness. This chapter explores how developers can enhance human connection through thoughtful design and innovative features.

The Responsibility of Developers

Developers are at the forefront of shaping our digital experiences. Every feature, interface, and interaction they create can either promote isolation or foster connection. Recognizing this responsibility is the first step toward designing for togetherness. Developers must understand that their work impacts the mental and emotional well-being of users. By prioritizing human connection, they can create technology that not only serves functional purposes but also enriches lives[1].

Principles of Designing for Togetherness

1. User-Centric Design

User-centric design focuses on creating products that meet the needs and preferences of users. For fostering human connection, this means understanding how users interact with each other and what they value in their social experiences. Conducting thorough user research, including interviews and surveys, can provide insights into these needs[2]. By empathizing with users, developers can design features that enhance their ability to connect meaningfully.

2. Encouraging Authentic Interactions

Authenticity is the foundation of meaningful connections. Developers can encourage authentic interactions by designing platforms that prioritize genuine engagement over superficial metrics. For instance, instead of emphasizing likes and follower counts, platforms can highlight meaningful conversations and shared experiences. Features such as long-form posts, personal stories, and collaborative projects can promote deeper connections[3].

3. Creating Safe Spaces

A sense of safety is essential for fostering genuine connections. Developers must prioritize user safety by implementing robust moderation tools and clear community guidelines. Features such as content filters, reporting mechanisms, and verified accounts can help create a trustworthy environment where users feel comfortable expressing themselves[4]. Additionally, privacy controls should be intuitive, allowing users to manage their personal information and interactions confidently.

4. Facilitating Group Dynamics

Group interactions can enhance a sense of community and belonging. Developers can design features that facilitate group dynamics, such as group chats, forums, and collaborative tools. These features should support various group sizes and types, from small friend circles to large interest-based communities. Integrating real-time collaboration tools, like shared documents and live video, can also strengthen group cohesion[5].

Case Studies in Designing for Togetherness

1. Social Media Platforms

Social media platforms have a significant influence on how we connect with others. Some platforms have made strides in fostering authentic connections. For example, Facebook's introduction of Groups has allowed users to form communities around shared interests and causes. These groups often become support networks where members can engage in meaningful discussions and share resources[6]. Similarly, Instagram's Close Friends feature lets users share content with a select group, promoting more intimate interactions[7].

2. Collaboration Tools

Tools designed for collaboration, such as Slack and Microsoft Teams, have also incorporated features that foster connection. These platforms go beyond work-related communication, offering channels for social interactions, hobby groups, and wellness activities. Features like virtual coffee breaks, shared calendars, and collaborative documents help create a sense of camaraderie among team members, even in remote settings[8].

3. Gaming Communities

Online gaming has long been a space for forming connections. Games like Fortnite and Animal Crossing incorporate social features that allow players to connect and collaborate. In Fortnite, players can team up and strategize together, building friendships through shared challenges. Animal Crossing emphasizes community-building, with players visiting each other's islands and participating in cooperative activities. These features transform gaming from a solitary activity into a social experience[9].

Innovative Features to Enhance Connection

1. Integrated Video and Voice Chat

Real-time communication tools like video and voice chat can significantly enhance online interactions. Developers can integrate these features seamlessly into their platforms, making it easy for users to switch from text-based communication to more personal interactions. For example, integrating video chat into messaging apps allows users to have face-to-face conversations without leaving the app[10].

2. Virtual Reality (VR) and Augmented Reality (AR)

VR and AR technologies offer immersive experiences that can bring people closer together. VR platforms like AltspaceVR and VRChat create virtual environments where users can interact as if they were in the same physical space. These technologies can be used for social events, meetings, and even casual hangouts, providing a sense of presence that traditional communication tools cannot match[11].

3. Social Wellness Features

Integrating wellness features into social platforms can promote healthier interactions. For instance, apps like Headspace and Calm offer guided meditations and mindfulness exercises that users can do together. Social fitness apps like Strava allow users to share their workout progress and motivate each other. These features support both mental and physical well-being, enhancing the overall sense of connection[12].

4. Localized Social Networks

Localized social networks focus on connecting people within specific geographic areas. Platforms like Nextdoor and Meetup facilitate local interactions, helping users find and engage with community events, local groups, and nearby friends. These networks strengthen community bonds and encourage offline meetups, fostering real-world connections[13].

Challenges and Ethical Considerations

1. Balancing Engagement and Well-Being

One of the primary challenges developers face is balancing user engagement with well-being. Features designed to keep users on the platform longer can sometimes lead to negative outcomes, such as addiction and burnout. Developers must strive to create engaging experiences that also promote healthy usage patterns. This can include implementing time limits, providing usage insights, and encouraging breaks[14].

2. Addressing Digital Divide

While designing for togetherness, developers must also consider the digital divide-the gap between those who have access to technology and those who do not.

Ensuring that platforms are accessible to a diverse range of users, including those with limited internet access or older devices, is crucial. Inclusive design practices, such as offering low-bandwidth versions and optimizing for accessibility, can help bridge this gap[15].

3. Ensuring Data Privacy and Security

Protecting user data is paramount in fostering trust and connection. Developers must prioritize data privacy and security by implementing strong encryption, transparent data practices, and user control over personal information. Users should feel confident that their data is protected and used responsibly, which in turn fosters a safer environment for connection[16].

Developers have a unique opportunity to shape the future of human connection through thoughtful and innovative design. By prioritizing user-centric design, authenticity, safety, and group dynamics, they can create digital experiences that bring people closer together. As we navigate the digital landscape, the intentional design for togetherness will be essential in transforming our online interactions into meaningful, real-world relationships. Through creativity and ethical responsibility, developers can make a profound impact on how we connect, support, and grow with each other in the digital age.

Exercise: Designing for Togetherness

This exercise is designed to help you apply the principles discussed in this chapter to enhance human connection through thoughtful design. Follow the steps below to integrate user-centric design, authenticity, safety, and group dynamics into your digital projects.

Step 1: Understanding Your Users

1. Conduct User Research

- Create a survey or interview guide to gather information about your users. Focus on their social interaction preferences, challenges they face in connecting with others, and what they value in online communities.

- Examples of questions:
✓ How do you currently use social media or digital platforms to connect with others?
✓ What features do you find most helpful for maintaining meaningful relationships online?
✓ What challenges do you face when trying to connect with people digitally?

2. Analyze the Data

- Collect and analyze the responses to identify common themes and insights. Look for patterns in user behavior and preferences that can inform your design process.

Step 2: Designing for Authentic Interactions

1. Develop Features that Promote Authenticity

- Based on your user research, brainstorm features that encourage genuine engagement. Examples include long-form posts, personal stories, and collaborative projects.
- Sketch or wireframe these features to visualize how they will look and function within your platform.

2. Create Prototypes

- Develop low-fidelity prototypes of the features you brainstormed. Use tools like Sketch, Figma, or Adobe XD to create interactive prototypes that you can test with users.

Step 3: Ensuring User Safety

1. Implement Moderation Tools

- Design and implement tools that help maintain a safe and respectful environment. These could include content filters, reporting mechanisms, and verified accounts.
- Ensure that these tools are easy to use and accessible to all users.

2. Establish Community Guidelines

- Draft clear and comprehensive community guidelines that outline acceptable behavior and the consequences for violations.
- Make these guidelines easily accessible and visible to all users.

Step 4: Facilitating Group Dynamics

1. Design Group Interaction Features

- Brainstorm features that facilitate group interactions, such as group chats, forums, and collaborative tools. Consider how these features can support various group sizes and types.

- Sketch or wireframe these group interaction features.

2. Prototype and Test

- Create prototypes of the group interaction features and test them with users. Gather feedback on usability and effectiveness in fostering group dynamics.

Step 5: Integrating Real-Time Communication Tools

1. Incorporate Video and Voice Chat

- Design and integrate real-time communication tools like video and voice chat into your platform. Ensure these features are seamlessly integrated and easy to access.
- Test these tools with users to ensure they enhance the user experience and foster deeper connections.

Step 6: Leveraging Emerging Technologies

1. Explore VR and AR Features

- Research how VR and AR technologies can be used to enhance human connection. Brainstorm potential applications for your platform, such as virtual meetups or augmented reality experiences.

- Create prototypes or mockups of these features and gather user feedback.

2. Develop a Pilot Program

- Develop a pilot program to test VR or AR features with a small group of users. Collect data on user experience, engagement, and the impact on connection.

Step 7: Promoting Social Wellness

1. Integrate Wellness Features

- Design features that promote social wellness, such as guided meditations, mindfulness exercises, and social fitness challenges.
- Prototype these features and test them with users to ensure they are engaging and beneficial.

2. Create a Wellness Program

- Develop a comprehensive wellness program that includes regular activities and challenges users can participate in. Encourage users to share their progress and experiences to foster a sense of community.

Step 8: Evaluating and Iterating

1. Collect Feedback

- Continuously collect feedback from users on the new features and their impact on connection. Use surveys, interviews, and analytics to gather data.
- Pay attention to both qualitative and quantitative feedback to get a holistic view of user experience.

2. Iterate and Improve

- Based on the feedback, make necessary adjustments to the features and overall design. Focus on enhancing usability, safety, and the ability to foster genuine connections.
- Iterate on the design and development process to continually improve the platform.

By following these steps, you will be able to design digital products that enhance human connection, foster authentic interactions, and create a sense of community. This exercise will help you apply the principles discussed in this chapter, leading to more meaningful and impactful digital experiences.

Chapter 14: Spiritual Solace: Reconnecting with Self and Nature

In a world teeming with digital distractions and ceaseless connectivity, it's easy to lose touch with ourselves and the natural world around us. Spiritual solace, the deep sense of peace and connection that arises from within, often feels elusive. Yet, it is in reconnecting with ourselves and nature that we can find true fulfillment and respite from the chaos of modern life. This chapter explores the importance of spiritual solace and offers practical steps to help you reconnect with yourself and nature.

The Importance of Spiritual Solace

Spiritual solace is more than a fleeting feeling of calm; it is a profound sense of alignment and harmony with the world. It transcends religious boundaries and speaks to our core need for meaning and connection. In the midst of our busy lives, this solace can be a grounding force, providing clarity and inner peace[1].

The Disconnection Dilemma

Our reliance on technology, while beneficial in many ways, has contributed to a growing sense of disconnection. Constant notifications, social media pressures, and the relentless pace of information can leave us feeling overwhelmed and isolated. This disconnection extends beyond our relationships with others; it affects our relationship with ourselves and the natural environment[2].

Reconnecting with Self

1. Mindfulness and Meditation

Mindfulness and meditation are powerful tools for reconnecting with yourself. These practices encourage you to be present in the moment, fostering self-awareness and inner peace. Start with a few minutes of meditation each day, focusing on your breath and letting go of distracting thoughts. Over time, increase the duration and explore different techniques, such as guided meditations or body scans[3].

2. Journaling

Journaling is an effective way to explore your thoughts and emotions. Set aside time each day to write about your experiences, aspirations, and challenges.

This practice helps you process your feelings and gain insights into your inner world. Reflecting on your journal entries over time can reveal patterns and growth, deepening your understanding of yourself[4].

3. Digital Detox

Taking regular breaks from technology is crucial for reconnecting with yourself. Designate specific times or days for a digital detox, during which you refrain from using digital devices. Use this time to engage in activities that nourish your soul, such as reading, painting, or simply relaxing. A digital detox can help you reset your mind and rediscover your interests and passions[5].

4. Self-Care Rituals

Incorporate self-care rituals into your daily routine. These rituals can be simple, such as taking a warm bath, practicing yoga, or spending time in nature. Prioritizing self-care helps you maintain a healthy balance and strengthens your connection with yourself. It is a reminder that you are worthy of care and attention[6].

Reconnecting with Nature

1. Nature Walks

Spending time in nature is a powerful way to reconnect with the world around you. Regular nature walks, whether in a park, forest, or beach, can help you appreciate the beauty and tranquility of the natural environment. Pay attention to the sights, sounds, and smells around you, and allow yourself to be fully present in the experience[7].

2. Gardening

Gardening is a therapeutic activity that allows you to connect with the earth. Whether you have a large garden or a small balcony, cultivating plants can bring a sense of accomplishment and joy. Gardening teaches patience and mindfulness, as you nurture and witness the growth of living things[8].

3. Outdoor Meditation

Combining meditation with the outdoors can enhance your practice. Find a quiet spot in nature where you can sit comfortably and meditate. The natural surroundings can deepen your sense of peace and connection, grounding you in the present moment. This practice can be particularly powerful at sunrise or sunset, when the beauty of nature is most striking[9].

4. Nature Retreats

Consider taking a nature retreat to immerse yourself fully in the natural world. Retreats offer an opportunity to disconnect from daily stresses and technology, allowing you to focus on inner growth and relaxation. Whether it's a weekend camping trip or a week-long stay at a secluded cabin, a nature retreat can rejuvenate your spirit and deepen your connection with the environment[10].

Integrating Spiritual Practices into Daily Life

1. Create a Sacred Space
Designate a space in your home for spiritual practices. This could be a corner with a meditation cushion, candles, and meaningful objects. Having a dedicated space reminds you to take time for yourself and fosters a sense of tranquility[11].

2. Morning Rituals

Start your day with a morning ritual that sets a positive tone. This could include meditation, stretching, or reading an inspiring book. Morning rituals help you begin the day with intention and mindfulness, grounding you before the demands of the day take over[12].

3. Gratitude Practice

Cultivating gratitude is a simple yet profound practice. Each day, take a moment to reflect on the things you are grateful for. This practice shifts your focus from what's lacking to the abundance in your life, fostering a positive outlook and deeper appreciation for the present moment[13].

4. Mindful Consumption

Be mindful of the media and content you consume. Choose books, music, and programs that uplift and inspire you. Limit exposure to negative news and social media, which can contribute to feelings of anxiety and disconnection. Mindful consumption nurtures your spirit and supports a balanced, positive mindset[14].

Building a Community

1. Join Like-Minded Groups

Connecting with others who share your interests and values can enhance your spiritual journey. Join local or online groups focused on meditation, nature conservation, or other spiritual practices. These communities provide support, encouragement, and opportunities to learn from others[15].

2. Attend Workshops and Classes

Participate in workshops and classes that align with your spiritual interests. Whether it's a meditation workshop, a nature photography class, or a yoga retreat, these experiences can deepen your practice and connect you with like-minded individuals[16].

3. Volunteer in Nature Conservation

Volunteering for nature conservation projects is a fulfilling way to give back to the environment. Activities such as tree planting, beach cleanups, and wildlife preservation not only benefit nature but also foster a sense of purpose and connection. Volunteering in nature can be a powerful reminder of our interconnectedness with the earth[17].

Reconnecting with yourself and nature is a journey of self-discovery and spiritual growth. In the hustle and bustle of modern life, it is essential to carve out time for practices that nurture your inner world and deepen your connection with the natural environment. By integrating mindfulness, self-care, and nature-based activities into your daily routine, you can find spiritual solace and a renewed sense of purpose. Embrace the journey of reconnection and let the beauty and tranquility of nature guide you back to yourself.

Exercise: Reconnecting with Self and Nature

This exercise is designed to help you apply the principles discussed in this chapter to reconnect with yourself and nature. By following these steps, you will deepen your understanding and implementation of mindfulness, self-care, and nature-based activities.

Step 1: Mindfulness and Meditation

1. Daily Meditation Practice

- Set aside 10-15 minutes each day for meditation. Find a quiet, comfortable place where you can sit undisturbed. Focus on your breath, observing each inhale and exhale.
- Gradually increase the duration of your meditation sessions as you become more comfortable with the practice.

2. Mindfulness Check-Ins

- Throughout the day, take short mindfulness breaks. Pause for a few minutes to focus on your breath, body sensations, or surroundings. This helps you stay present and aware.

Step 2: Journaling

1. Daily Journaling

- Spend 10 minutes each day writing in a journal. Reflect on your thoughts, feelings, and experiences. Use prompts such as:
- What am I grateful for today?
- What challenges did I face, and how did I overcome them?
- What did I learn about myself today?

2. Weekly Review

- At the end of each week, review your journal entries. Look for patterns, insights, and areas of growth. Write a summary of your reflections and any goals for the following week.

Step 3: Digital Detox

1. Schedule Digital Detox Periods

- Choose specific times or days for a digital detox. During these periods, refrain from using digital devices such as phones, computers, and tablets.

- Use this time to engage in offline activities that bring you joy and relaxation, such as reading, hiking, or spending time with loved ones.

2. **Reflect on Your Experience**

- After each digital detox, write a journal entry about your experience. Consider the following questions:
✓ How did I feel without digital distractions?
✓ What activities did I enjoy the most?
✓ What did I learn about my relationship with technology?

Step 4: Self-Care Rituals

1. Develop a Self-Care Routine

✓ Create a self-care routine that includes activities you find relaxing and fulfilling. This could include practices such as yoga, taking a warm bath, or engaging in a creative hobby.
✓ Schedule these activities into your daily or weekly routine, making self-care a priority.

2. **Track Your Self-Care Practices**

   ✓ Keep a self-care journal to track your activities and how they make you feel. Note any changes in your mood, energy levels, and overall well-being.

Step 5: Reconnecting with Nature

1. Nature Walks
- Plan regular nature walks in your local area. Choose parks, forests, or beaches where you can immerse yourself in the natural environment.
- During your walks, practice mindfulness by paying attention to the sights, sounds, and smells around you. Allow yourself to be fully present in the moment.

2. Gardening

- Start a small garden, whether it's in your backyard, balcony, or a community garden. Choose plants that you enjoy and that suit your environment.
- Spend time each day caring for your plants, observing their growth, and appreciating the life you're nurturing.

3. **Outdoor Meditation**

- Find a quiet spot in nature where you can sit comfortably and meditate. Focus on the natural surroundings, using the sights and sounds to deepen your meditation practice.
- Try this practice at different times of the day, such as sunrise or sunset, to experience the changing beauty of nature.

4. **Nature Retreats**

- Plan a nature retreat to fully immerse yourself in the natural world. This could be a weekend camping trip, a visit to a secluded cabin, or a stay at a retreat center focused on nature and mindfulness.
- Use this time to disconnect from technology and daily stresses, focusing on inner growth and relaxation.

Step 6: Integrating Spiritual Practices into Daily Life

1. Create a Sacred Space

Designate a space in your home for spiritual practices. Include items that inspire tranquility and mindfulness, such as a meditation cushion, candles, and meaningful objects.

Spend time in this space daily, engaging in practices such as meditation, journaling, or reading spiritual texts.

2. Morning Rituals

- Develop a morning ritual that sets a positive tone for your day. This could include activities like meditation, stretching, or reading an inspiring book.
- Consistently practice your morning ritual to cultivate mindfulness and intention at the start of each day.

3. Gratitude Practice

- Each day, take a moment to reflect on the things you are grateful for. Write down at least three things in a gratitude journal.
- Review your gratitude entries regularly to remind yourself of the abundance in your life and to foster a positive outlook.

4. Mindful Consumption

- Be mindful of the media and content you consume. Choose books, music, and programs that uplift and inspire you.
- Limit exposure to negative news and social media, which can contribute to feelings of anxiety and disconnection.

Step 7: Building a Community

1. Join Like-Minded Groups

- Find local or online groups that share your interests and values, such as meditation, nature conservation, or spiritual practices.
- Participate actively in these communities, attending events, contributing to discussions, and supporting others.

2. Attend Workshops and Classes

- Sign up for workshops and classes that align with your spiritual interests. This could include meditation workshops, nature photography classes, or yoga retreats.
- Use these opportunities to deepen your practice and connect with like-minded individuals.

3. Volunteer in Nature Conservation

- Get involved in nature conservation projects, such as tree planting, beach cleanups, or wildlife preservation.
- Volunteering not only benefits the environment but also fosters a sense of purpose and connection with nature.

By following these steps, you will be able to reconnect with yourself and nature, finding spiritual solace and a renewed sense of purpose. This exercise will help you implement the concepts discussed in this chapter, leading to a more balanced, fulfilling life.

NOTES:

Conclusion: Embracing Our Humanity in the Age of Technology

As we reach the conclusion of this journey through the intricacies of loneliness and connection in the digital age, it's time to reflect on the lessons we've learned and envision a future where technology enhances our humanity rather than diminishes it. Throughout this book, we've explored how technology has reshaped our interactions, both positively and negatively. Now, we must consider how to integrate these insights into our daily lives to foster genuine connections and a sense of belonging.

The Dual Nature of Technology

Technology is a double-edged sword. On one hand, it has provided us with unprecedented access to information, instant communication, and the ability to connect with people across the globe.

On the other hand, it has also contributed to feelings of isolation, superficial interactions, and a disconnect from our immediate surroundings and inner selves. Acknowledging this dual nature is crucial in our quest to harness technology for the betterment of our social and emotional well-being.

Reflecting on Key Lessons

1. Mindful Technology Use

One of the most significant takeaways from this book is the importance of mindful technology use. By setting clear intentions, creating boundaries, and regularly disconnecting from our devices, we can reclaim control over our digital lives. Mindfulness in technology use encourages us to be present in our interactions, whether online or offline, fostering deeper and more meaningful connections.

2. Authenticity in Digital Interactions

Authenticity is the cornerstone of genuine relationships. In a world where social media often promotes curated and idealized versions of life, striving for authenticity can be a powerful antidote. Sharing our true selves, vulnerabilities, and real experiences not only strengthens our connections with others but also enhances our own sense of self-worth and belonging.

3. Balancing Online and Offline Relationships

While digital connections are valuable, they should complement, not replace, our offline relationships. Transitioning from online interactions to real-world meetings can deepen bonds and create lasting memories. Whether it's meeting an online friend for coffee or attending community events, integrating our digital and physical worlds is essential for a balanced and fulfilling social life.

4. Designing Technology for Human Connection

Developers and tech companies have a profound responsibility in shaping the digital landscape. By prioritizing user-centric design, fostering safe and inclusive spaces, and promoting features that encourage meaningful interactions, technology can become a bridge rather than a barrier to connection. Innovations such as integrated video chat, virtual reality environments, and social wellness tools can help bring people closer together in authentic ways.

5. Reconnecting with Nature and Self

In our fast-paced, digitally-driven lives, it's easy to lose touch with ourselves and the natural world. Practices such as mindfulness, journaling, and spending time in nature are vital for grounding us in the present moment and nurturing our inner peace. Reconnecting with nature and self helps us find balance, reduce stress, and cultivate a deeper sense of belonging and purpose.

Envisioning a Connected Future

As we look to the future, it's clear that technology will continue to evolve and shape our lives in ways we cannot yet fully imagine. However, by embracing the principles discussed in this book, we can ensure that this evolution leads to greater human connection rather than increased isolation. Here are some key visions for a connected future:

1. Human-Centered Technology

The future of technology should be human-centered, focusing on enhancing well-being and fostering genuine connections. This means designing digital tools that prioritize mental health, inclusivity, and real-world interactions. By keeping human needs at the forefront, technology can become a powerful ally in our quest for connection and fulfillment.

2. Digital Literacy and Mindfulness Education

Promoting digital literacy and mindfulness education from an early age can equip future generations with the skills to navigate the digital world responsibly. Teaching young people about the impact of technology on mental health, the importance of authenticity, and the value of offline relationships can create a more balanced and connected society.

3. Community-Driven Innovation

Innovations in technology should be driven by community needs and values. By involving diverse voices in the design and development process, tech companies can create products that truly resonate with users and foster a sense of belonging. Community-driven innovation ensures that technology serves the collective good and enhances human connection.

A Call to Action

As we conclude this exploration, it's time to turn insights into action. Here are practical steps you can take to foster genuine connections in your life:

1. Practice Mindful Technology Use

- Set specific goals for how you want to use technology.
- Create tech-free zones and times in your daily routine.
- Regularly disconnect from digital devices to engage in offline activities.
-

2. Cultivate Authentic Relationships

- Share your true self in both online and offline interactions.
- Foster deep conversations and meaningful connections.

- Prioritize face-to-face interactions to strengthen relationships.

3. Engage in Community and Nature

- Join local or online groups that align with your interests and values.
- Participate in community events and volunteer activities.
- Spend regular time in nature to reconnect with the environment and yourself.

4. Advocate for Human-Centered Technology

- Support tech companies that prioritize user well-being and genuine connection.
- Provide feedback to developers and advocate for features that enhance community and authenticity.
- Stay informed about digital literacy and mindfulness education initiatives.

Moving Forward Together

The journey to fostering genuine connections in a digitally dominated world is ongoing. It requires continuous reflection, adjustment, and intentionality. By integrating the insights and practices discussed in this book, you can navigate the digital landscape more mindfully, creating deeper, more meaningful relationships that enrich your life.

As you move forward, remember that connection starts with you. By nurturing your inner world, embracing authenticity, and engaging with others mindfully, you can bridge the digital divide and foster a sense of togetherness that transcends screens and devices. This journey is not just about technology; it's about reclaiming our humanity in a world that often feels disconnected. Embrace this path with an open heart, and let the power of genuine connection transform your life.

Final Thought

In a planet full of people, you are not alone. By taking intentional steps to connect deeply with yourself, nature, and others, you can overcome the loneliness that technology sometimes brings. Together, we can create a world where technology enhances, rather than diminishes, our human connections. Start today, and watch as your life fills with the richness of genuine, meaningful relationships.

FOOTNOTES

Part I: Understanding Our Loneliness

Chapter 01: The Evolution of Communication: From Face-to-Face to Digital Interfaces

[1] Tomasello, M. (2008). *Origins of Human Communication*. MIT Press.

[2] Dunbar, R. I. M. (1996). *Grooming, Gossip, and the Evolution of Language*. Harvard University Press.

[3] Robinson, A. (2007). *The Story of Writing: Alphabets, Hieroglyphs, and Pictograms*. Thames & Hudson.

[4] Goody, J. (1986). *The Logic of Writing and the Organization of Society*. Cambridge University Press.

[5] Eisenstein, E. L. (1980). *The Printing Press as an Agent of Change*. Cambridge University Press.

[6] Febvre, L., & Martin, H.-J. (1976). *The Coming of the Book: The Impact of Printing 1450–1800*. Verso.

[7] Habermas, J. (1989). *The Structural Transformation of the Public Sphere: An Inquiry into a Category of Bourgeois Society*. MIT Press.

[8] Briggs, A., & Burke, P. (2009). *A Social History of the Media: From Gutenberg to the Internet*. Polity.

[9] Standage, T. (1998). *The Victorian Internet: The Remarkable Story of the Telegraph and the Nineteenth Century's On-line Pioneers*. Walker & Company.

[10] Huurdeman, A. A. (2003). *The Worldwide History of Telecommunications*. Wiley-IEEE Press.

[11] Headrick, D. R. (1991). *The Invisible Weapon: Telecommunications and International Politics 1851–1945*. Oxford University Press.

[12] Blondheim, M. (1994). *News Over the Wires: The Telegraph and the Flow of Public Information in America, 1844-1897*. Harvard University Press.

[13] Fischer, C. S. (1992). *America Calling: A Social History of the Telephone to 1940*. University of California Press.

[14] Bellis, M. (2021). *"The Invention and History of the Telephone"*. ThoughtCo. Retrieved from [link].

[15] Casson, H. N. (1910). *The History of the Telephone*. A. C. McClurg & Co.

[16] Marvin, C. (1988). *When Old Technologies Were New: Thinking About Electric Communication in the Late Nineteenth Century*. Oxford University Press.

[17] Fischer, C. S. (1994). *America Calling: A Social History of the Telephone to 1940*. University of California Press.

[18] Leiner, B. M., Cerf, V. G., Clark, D. D., Kahn, R. E., Kleinrock, L., Lynch, D. C., ... & Wolff, S. (1997). "The Past and Future History of the Internet". Communications of the ACM, 40(2), 102-108.

[19] Abbate, J. (1999). *Inventing the Internet*. MIT Press.

[20] Smith, R. E. (2008). *Email in the 21st Century: The Communication Tool That Should Be Regulated*. ABC-CLIO.

[21] Baron, N. S. (2008). *Always On: Language in an Online and Mobile World*. Oxford University Press.

[22] Rheingold, H. (2000). *The Virtual Community: Homesteading on the Electronic Frontier*. MIT Press.

[23] Kaplan, A. M., & Haenlein, M. (2010). "Users of the World, Unite! The Challenges and Opportunities of Social Media". Business Horizons, 53(1), 59-68.

[24] Ellison, N. B., & Boyd, D. (2013). "Sociality through Social Network Sites". In Dutton, W. H. (Ed.), The Oxford Handbook of Internet Studies. Oxford University Press.

[25] Turkle, S. (2011). *Alone Together: Why We Expect More from Technology and Less from Each Other*. Basic Books.

[26] Derks, D., Fischer, A. H., & Bos, A. E. (2008). "The Role of Emotion in Computer-Mediated Communication: A Review". Computers in Human Behavior, 24(3), 766-785.

[27] Kross, E., Verduyn, P., Demiralp, E., Park, J., Lee, D. S., Lin, N., ... & Ybarra, O. (2013). "Facebook Use Predicts Declines in Subjective Well-Being in Young Adults". PLOS One, 8(8), e69841.

[28] Lin, L. Y., Sidani, J. E., Shensa, A., Radovic, A., Miller, E., Colditz, J. B., ... & Primack, B. A. (2016). "Association Between Social Media Use and Depression Among U.S. Young Adults". Depression and Anxiety, 33(4), 323-331.

[29] Johnson, R. (2020). "How Zoom Became the Hero of the Pandemic". The New York Times. Retrieved from [link].

[30] Smith, A. (2020). "How the Pandemic Is Changing Digital Communication". Harvard Business Review. Retrieved from [link].

[31] Bailenson, J. N. (2018). Experience on Demand: What Virtual Reality Is, How It Works, and What It Can Do. W. W. Norton & Company.

[32] Turkle, S. (2015). *Reclaiming Conversation: The Power of Talk in a Digital Age*. Penguin Books.

[33] Hampton, K. N., & Wellman, B. (2003). "Neighboring in Netville: How the Internet Supports Community and Social Capital in a Wired Suburb". City & Community, 2(4), 277-311.

[34] Putnam, R. D. (2000). *Bowling Alone: The Collapse and Revival of American Community*. Simon & Schuster.

[35] Coleman, J. S. (1988). "Social Capital in the Creation of Human Capital". American Journal of Sociology, 94, S95-S120.

Chapter 02: The Illusion of Connectedness: Social Media's False Promises

[1] Faraone, Stephen V., et al. "The Dopamine Reward Pathway in ADHD." *Frontiers in Neuroscience*, vol. 13, 2019, p. 111.

[2] Turkle, Sherry. *Reclaiming Conversation: The Power of Talk in a Digital Age*. Penguin Books, 2015.

[3] Goffman, Erving. *The Presentation of Self in Everyday Life*. Doubleday, 1959.

[4] Twenge, Jean M., et al. "Increases in Depressive Symptoms, Suicide-Related Outcomes, and Suicide Rates Among U.S. Adolescents After 2010 and Links to Increased New Media Screen Time." *Clinical Psychological Science*, vol. 6, no. 1, 2018, pp. 3-17.

[5] Przybylski, Andrew K., et al. "Motivational, Emotional, and Behavioral Correlates of Fear of Missing Out." *Computers in Human Behavior*, vol. 29, no. 4, 2013, pp. 1841-1848.

[6] Alter, Adam. *Irresistible: The Rise of Addictive Technology and the Business of Keeping Us Hooked*. Penguin Press, 2017.

[7] Schwartz, Barry. *The Paradox of Choice: Why More Is Less*. Harper Perennial, 2004.

[8] Carr, Nicholas. *The Shallows: What the Internet Is Doing to Our Brains*. W. W. Norton & Company, 2010.

[9] Boyd, Danah. *It's Complicated: The Social Lives of Networked Teens*. Yale University Press, 2014.

[10] Lanier, Jaron. *Ten Arguments for Deleting Your Social Media Accounts Right Now*. Henry Holt and Co., 2018.

[11] Newport, Cal. *Digital Minimalism: Choosing a Focused Life in a Noisy World*. Portfolio, 2019.

[12] Turkle, Sherry. *Alone Together: Why We Expect More from Technology and Less from Each Other*. Basic Books, 2011.

[13] Rheingold, Howard. *Net Smart: How to Thrive Online*. MIT Press, 2012.

[14] Putnam, Robert D. *Bowling Alone: The Collapse and Revival of American Community*. Simon & Schuster, 2000.

[15] Price, Catherine. *How to Break Up with Your Phone: The 30-Day Plan to Take Back Your Life*. Ten Speed Press, 2018.

[16] Brown, Brené. *Daring Greatly: How the Courage to Be Vulnerable Transforms the Way We Live, Love, Parent, and Lead*. Gotham Books, 2012.

Chapter 03: Connecting Across Landscapes: Technology's Impact on Social Bonds in Urban, Suburban, and Rural Areas

[1] Fischer, Claude S. "The Urban Experience: A People Environment Perspective." Cities and Social Bonds, vol. 2, no. 3, 2011, pp. 245-263.

[2] Hampton, Keith N., et al. "Social Media and Social Isolation among Older Adults." Information, Communication & Society, vol. 21, no. 9, 2018, pp. 115-134.

[3] Turkle, Sherry. *Alone Together: Why We Expect More from Technology and Less from Each Other*. Basic Books, 2012.

[4] Simmel, Georg. "The Metropolis and Mental Life." Sociology of Urban Life, edited by Leo Snell, Macmillan, 1950, pp. 10-20.

[5] Putnam, Robert D. *Bowling Alone: The Collapse and Revival of American Community*. Simon & Schuster, 2000.

[6] Wellman, Barry. "Physical Place and Cyberplace: The Rise of Personalized Networking." International Journal of Urban and Regional Research, vol. 25, no. 2, 2001, pp. 227-252.

[7] Blanchard, Anita L., and Tom Horan. "Virtual Communities and Social Capital." Social Science Computer Review, vol. 16, no. 3, 1998, pp. 293-307.

[8] Mesch, Gustavo S. "Social Relationships and Internet Use among Adolescents in Israel." Social Science Quarterly, vol. 80, no. 2, 1999, pp. 329-339.

[9] Glasgow, Nina. "Older Rural Adults and Their Caregivers." Aging in Rural America, edited by Howard E. Hamilton, Springer, 2012, pp. 57-75.

[10] McGrath, John. "Internet Access and Use in Rural Areas." Journal of Rural Studies, vol. 15, no. 3, 1999, pp. 365-374.

[11] Whitacre, Brian E., et al. "Broadband's Contribution to Economic Health in Rural Areas: A Causal Analysis." Telecommunications Policy, vol. 38, no. 11, 2014, pp. 837-846.

[12] Selwyn, Neil. "The Information Aged: A Qualitative Study of Older Adults' Use of Information and Communications Technology." Journal of Aging Studies, vol. 18, no. 4, 2004, pp. 369-384.

[13] McPherson, Miller, et al. "Social Isolation in America: Changes in Core Discussion Networks over Two Decades." American Sociological Review, vol. 71, no. 3, 2006, pp. 353-375.

[14] DiMaggio, Paul, et al. "The Digital Divide: Inequality in Internet Access and Use." Annual Review of Sociology, vol. 27, 2001, pp. 307-336.

[15] Boyd, Danah. It's Complicated: The Social Lives of Networked Teens. Yale University Press, 2014.

[16] Rainie, Lee, and Barry Wellman. Networked: The New Social Operating System. MIT Press, 2012.

[17] Putnam, Robert D., and Lewis Feldstein. Better Together: Restoring the American Community. Simon & Schuster, 2004.

[18] Preece, Jennifer J. "Online Communities: Designing Usability, Supporting Sociability." Journal of Computer-Mediated Communication, vol. 10, no. 4, 2005, pp. 1-27.

[19] Turkle, Sherry. Reclaiming Conversation: The Power of Talk in a Digital Age. Penguin Press, 2015.

[20] Warschauer, Mark. Technology and Social Inclusion: Rethinking the Digital Divide. MIT Press, 2003.

[21] Fiesler, Casey, and Amy S. Bruckman. "Ethics for Studying Online Communities." Internet Research Ethics for the Social Age, edited by Michael Zimmer, et al., Peter Lang, 2017, pp. 217-235.

[22] Ling, Rich. New Tech, New Ties: How Mobile Communication Is Reshaping Social Cohesion. MIT Press, 2008.

[23] Wright, Kevin B., et al. "The Online Support Group Experience: A Qualitative Study of Communication Practices and Motivations." Journal of Computer-Mediated Communication, vol. 10, no. 4, 2005, pp. 1-26.

Chapter 04: "The Psychology of Loneliness: Recognizing the Inner Signs

[1] Hawkley, L. C., & Cacioppo, J. T. (2010). "Loneliness Matters: A Theoretical and Empirical Review of Consequences and Mechanisms". Annals of Behavioral Medicine, 40(2), 218-227.

[2] Lim, M. H., Rodebaugh, T. L., Zyphur, M. J., & Gleeson, J. F. (2016). "Loneliness Over Time: The Crucial Role of Social Anxiety". Journal of Abnormal Psychology, 125(5), 620-630.

[3] Leary, M. R. (1990). "Responses to Social Exclusion: Social Anxiety, Jealousy, Loneliness, Depression, and Low Self-Esteem". Journal of Social and Clinical Psychology, 9(2), 221-229.

[4] Mikulincer, M., & Shaver, P. R. (2007). "Attachment in Adulthood: Structure, Dynamics, and Change". Guilford Press.

[5] Victor, C. R., Scambler, S. J., Bowling, A., & Bond, J. (2005). "The Prevalence of, and Risk Factors for, Loneliness in Later Life: A Survey of Older People in Great Britain". Ageing and Society, 25(6), 357-375.

[6] Cacioppo, J. T., & Patrick, W. (2008). Loneliness: Human Nature and the Need for Social Connection. W. W. Norton & Company.

[7] Heinrich, L. M., & Gullone, E. (2006). "The Clinical Significance of Loneliness: A Literature Review". Clinical Psychology Review, 26(6), 695-718.

[8] Nolen-Hoeksema, S., Wisco, B. E., & Lyubomirsky, S. (2008). "Rethinking Rumination". Perspectives on Psychological Science, 3(5), 400-424.

[9] Qualter, P., Vanhalst, J., Harris, R., Van Roekel, E., Lodder, G., Bangee, M., & Verhagen, M. (2015). "Loneliness Across the Life Span". Perspectives on Psychological Science, 10(2), 250-264.

[10] Hawkley, L. C., Thisted, R. A., & Cacioppo, J. T. (2009). "Loneliness Predicts Reduced Physical Activity: Cross-Sectional & Longitudinal Analyses". Health Psychology, 28(3), 354-363.

[11] Cacioppo, J. T., Hughes, M. E., Waite, L. J., Hawkley, L. C., & Thisted, R. A. (2006). "Loneliness as a Specific Risk Factor for Depressive Symptoms: Cross-Sectional and Longitudinal Analyses". Psychology and Aging, 21(1), 140-151.

[12] Beutel, M. E., Klein, E. M., Brähler, E., Reiner, I., Jünger, C., Michal, M., ... & Tibubos, A. N. (2017). "Loneliness in the General Population: Prevalence, Determinants and Relations to Mental Health". BMC Psychiatry, 17(1), 1-7.

[13] Cacioppo, J. T., & Hawkley, L. C. (2009). "Perceived Social Isolation and Cognition". Trends in Cognitive Sciences, 13(10), 447-454.

[14] Holt-Lunstad, J., Smith, T. B., & Layton, J. B. (2010). "Social Relationships and Mortality Risk: A Meta-analytic Review". PLOS Medicine, 7(7), e1000316.

[15] Masi, C. M., Chen, H. Y., Hawkley, L. C., & Cacioppo, J. T. (2011). "A Meta-Analysis of Interventions to Reduce Loneliness". Personality and Social Psychology Review, 15(3), 219-266.

[16] Neff, K. D. (2003). "Self-Compassion: An Alternative Conceptualization of a Healthy Attitude Toward Oneself". Self and Identity, 2(2), 85-101.

[17] Steger, M. F., Oishi, S., & Kashdan, T. B. (2009). "Meaning in Life Across the Life Span: Levels and Correlates of Meaning in Life from Emerging Adulthood to Older Adulthood". The Journal of Positive Psychology, 4(1), 43-52.

[18] Nowland, R., Necka, E. A., & Cacioppo, J. T. (2018). "Loneliness and Social Internet Use: Pathways to Reconnection in a Digital World?". Perspectives on Psychological Science, 13(1), 70-87.

Part II: The Irony of Technology-Induced Isolation

Chapter 05: When Phones Replace Humans: The Impact of Screen Time on Personal Relationships

[1] Smith, A. (2018). "The smartphone is the most transformative invention of the 21st century". Pew Research Center. Retrieved from https://www.pewresearch.org.

[2] Roberts, J. A., & David, M. E. (2016). "My life has become a major distraction from my cell phone: Partner phubbing and relationship satisfaction among romantic partners". Computers in Human Behavior, 54, 134-141.

[3] Przybylski, A. K., & Weinstein, N. (2013). "Can you connect with me now? How the presence of mobile communication technology influences face-to-face conversation quality". Journal of Social and Personal Relationships, 30(3), 325-335.

[4] Roberts, J. A., & David, M. E. (2016). "My life has become a major distraction from my cell phone: Partner phubbing and relationship satisfaction among romantic partners". Computers in Human Behavior, 54, 134-141.

[5] Przybylski, A. K., & Weinstein, N. (2013). "Can you connect with me now? How the presence of mobile communication technology influences face-to-face conversation quality". Journal of Social and Personal Relationships, 30(3), 325-335

[6] Misra, S., Cheng, L., Genevie, J., & Yuan, M. (2016). "The iPhone effect: The quality of in-person social interactions in the presence of mobile devices". Environment and Behavior, 48(2), 275-298.

[7] Konrath, S. H., O'Brien, E. H., & Hsing, C. (2011). "Changes in dispositional empathy in American college students over time: A meta-analysis". Personality and Social Psychology Review, 15(2), 180-198.

[8] Roberts, J. A., & David, M. E. (2016). "My life has become a major distraction from my cell phone: Partner phubbing and relationship satisfaction among romantic partners". Computers in Human Behavior, 54, 134-141.

[9] Twenge, J. M., & Campbell, W. K. (2018). "Associations between screen time and lower psychological well-being among children and adolescents: Evidence from a population-based study". Preventive Medicine Reports, 12, 271-283.

[10] McDaniel, B. T., & Coyne, S. M. (2016). ""Technoference": The interference of technology in couple relationships and implications for women's personal and relational well-being". Psychology of Popular Media Culture, 5(1), 85-98.

[11] Roberts, J. A., & David, M. E. (2016). "My life has become a major distraction from my cell phone: Partner phubbing and relationship satisfaction among romantic partners". Computers in Human Behavior, 54, 134-141.

[12] Misra, S., Cheng, L., Genevie, J., & Yuan, M. (2016). "The iPhone effect: The quality of in-person social interactions in the presence of mobile devices". Environment and Behavior, 48(2), 275-298.

[13] Kabat-Zinn, J. (1994). Wherever you go, there you are: Mindfulness meditation in everyday life. Hyperion.

[14] Turkle, S. (2017). Reclaiming conversation: The power of talk in a digital age. Penguin Books.

[15] Przybylski, A. K., & Weinstein, N. (2013). "Can you connect with me now? How the presence of mobile communication technology influences face-to-face conversation quality". Journal of Social and Personal Relationships, 30(3), 325-335.

[16] McDaniel, B. T., & Coyne, S. M. (2016). ""Technoference": The interference of technology in couple relationships and implications for women's personal and relational well-being". Psychology of Popular Media Culture, 5(1), 85-98.

[17] Roberts, J. A., & David, M. E. (2016). "My life has become a major distraction from my cell phone: Partner phubbing and relationship satisfaction among romantic partners". Computers in Human Behavior, 54, 134-141.

[18] Kabat-Zinn, J. (1994). Wherever you go, there you are: Mindfulness meditation in everyday life. Hyperion.

[19] Twenge, J. M., & Campbell, W. K. (2018). "Associations between screen time and lower psychological well-being among children and adolescents: Evidence from a population-based study". Preventive Medicine Reports, 12, 271-283.

[20] Konrath, S. H., O'Brien, E. H., & Hsing, C. (2011). "Changes in dispositional empathy in American college students over time: A meta-analysis". Personality and Social Psychology Review, 15(2), 180-198.

[21] Misra, S., Cheng, L., Genevie, J., & Yuan, M. (2016). "The iPhone effect: The quality of in-person social interactions in the presence of mobile devices". Environment and Behavior, 48(2), 275-298.

Chapter 06: The End of Privacy: How Constant Connectivity Can Create Distance

[1] Papacharissi, Z. (2010). A Private Sphere: Democracy in a Digital Age. Polity Press.

[2] Marwick, A. E., & boyd, d. (2014). "Networked privacy: How teenagers negotiate context in social media". New Media & Society, 16(7), 1051-1067.

[3] Turkle, S. (2011). Alone Together: Why We Expect More from Technology and Less from Each Other. Basic Books.

[4] Tufekci, Z. (2017). Twitter and Tear Gas: The Power and Fragility of Networked Protest. Yale University Press.

[5] Fuchs, C. (2011). "New Media, Web 2.0 and Surveillance". Sociological Compass, 5(2), 134-147.

[6] Przybylski, A. K., Murayama, K., DeHaan, C. R., & Gladwell, V. (2013). "Motivational, emotional, and behavioral correlates of fear of missing out". Computers in Human Behavior, 29(4), 1841-1848.

[7] Chou, H. T. G., & Edge, N. (2012). "They are happier and having better lives than I am: The impact of using Facebook on perceptions of others' lives". Cyberpsychology, Behavior, and Social Networking, 15(2), 117-121.

[8] Boyd, d. (2014). It's Complicated: The Social Lives of Networked Teens. Yale University Press.

[9] Suttie, J. (2019). "How to Cultivate Meaningful Connections Offline". Greater Good Magazine. Retrieved from https://greatergood.berkeley.edu.

[10] Roberts, J. A., & David, M. E. (2020). "The Social Media See-Saw: Positive and Negative Influences on Adolescents' Affective Well-Being". Teens and Technology.

[11] Neff, K. D. (2011). Self-Compassion: The Proven Power of Being Kind to Yourself. William Morrow.

[12] Harris, F. M., & Jones, S. R. (2019). "Understanding the Impact of Digital Media on Mental Health and Well-Being". Journal of Adolescent Health, 65(6), 700-703.

Chapter 07: Echo Chambers and Filter Bubbles: Losing the Human Touch

[1] Sunstein, C. R. (2001). Echo Chambers: Bush v. Gore, Impeachment, and Beyond. Princeton University Press.

[2] Pariser, E. (2011). The Filter Bubble: How the New Personalized Web Is Changing What We Read and How We Think. Penguin Press.

[3] Nickerson, R. S. (1998). "Confirmation Bias: A Ubiquitous Phenomenon in Many Guises". Review of General Psychology, 2(2), 175-220.

[4] Garrett, R. K. (2009). "Echo chambers online? Politically motivated selective exposure among Internet news users". Journal of Computer-Mediated Communication, 14(2), 265-285.

[5] Sunstein, C. R. (2018). #Republic: Divided Democracy in the Age of Social Media. Princeton University Press.

[6] Turkle, S. (2011). Alone Together: Why We Expect More from Technology and Less from Each Other. Basic Books.

[7] Bail, C. A., Argyle, L. P., Brown, T. W., Bumpus, J. P., Chen, H., Hunzaker, M. B. F., ... & Volfovsky, A. (2018). "Exposure to opposing views on social media can increase political polarization". Proceedings of the National Academy of Sciences, 115(37), 9216-9221.

[8] Iyengar, S., & Westwood, S. J. (2015). "Fear and loathing across party lines: New evidence on group polarization". American Journal of Political Science, 59(3), 690-707.

[9] Guess, A., Nyhan, B., & Reifler, J. (2018). "Selective exposure to misinformation: Evidence from the consumption of fake news during the 2016 US presidential campaign". European Research Council.

[10] Coleman, S. (2013). How Voters Feel. Cambridge University Press.

[11] Bakshy, E., Messing, S., & Adamic, L. A. (2015). "Exposure to ideologically diverse news and opinion on Facebook". Science, 348(6239), 1130-1132.

[12] Kahneman, D. (2011). Thinking, Fast and Slow. Farrar, Straus and Giroux.

[13] Pariser, E. (2011). The Filter Bubble: How the New Personalized Web Is Changing What We Read and How We Think. Penguin Press.

[14] Dunbar, R. I. M. (2016). "Do online social media cut through the constraints that limit the size of offline social networks?". Royal Society Open Science, 3(1), 150292.

[15] Davis, M. H. (1996). Empathy: A Social Psychological Approach. Westview Press.

[16] Putnam, R. D. (2000). Bowling Alone: The Collapse and Revival of American Community. Simon & Schuster.

[17] Brown, B. (2012). Daring Greatly: How the Courage to Be Vulnerable Transforms the Way We Live, Love, Parent, and Lead. Gotham Books.

Part III: Technology as a Bridge, Not a Barrier

Chapter 08: Digital Tools for Real Connection: The Positive Side of Tech

[1] Ellison, N. B., Vitak, J., Gray, R., & Lampe, C. (2014). "Cultivating social resources on social network sites: Facebook relationship maintenance behaviors and their role in social capital processes". Journal of Computer-Mediated Communication, 19(4), 855-870.

[2] Church, K., & de Oliveira, R. (2013). "What's up with WhatsApp? Comparing mobile instant messaging behaviors with traditional SMS". Proceedings of the 15th international conference on Human-computer interaction with mobile devices and services, 352-361.

[3] Zhang, R. (2016). "The stress-buffering effect of self-disclosure on Facebook: An examination of stressful life events, social support, and mental health among college students". Computers in Human Behavior, 75, 527-537.

[4] Gilbert, E., & Karahalios, K. (2009). "Predicting tie strength with social media". Proceedings of the SIGCHI Conference on Human Factors in Computing Systems, 211-220.

[5] Hartzog, P. (2007). "The commons as an emerging mode of social organization in the information age". Information, Communication & Society, 10(6), 766-785.

[6] Finkel, E. J., Eastwick, P. W., Karney, B. R., Reis, H. T., & Sprecher, S. (2012). "Online dating: A critical analysis from the perspective of psychological science". Psychological Science in the Public Interest, 13(1), 3-66.

[7] Firth, J., Torous, J., Nicholas, J., Carney, R., Pratap, A., Rosenbaum, S., & Sarris, J. (2017). "The efficacy of smartphone-based mental health interventions for depressive symptoms: a meta-analysis of randomized controlled trials". World Psychiatry, 16(3), 287-298.

[8] Richards, D., & Viganó, N. (2013). "Online counseling: A narrative and critical review of the literature". Journal of Clinical Psychology, 69(9), 994-1011.

[9] DeAndrea, D. C., & Walther, J. B. (2011). "Attributions for inconsistencies between online and offline self-presentations". Communication Research, 38(6), 805-825.

[10] Boyd, D. M., & Ellison, N. B. (2007). "Social network sites: Definition, history, and scholarship". Journal of Computer-Mediated Communication, 13(1), 210-230.

[11] Mazman, S. G., & Usluel, Y. K. (2010). "Modeling educational usage of Facebook". Computers & Education, 55(2), 444-453.

[12] Yu, J., & Liu, Y. (2020). "Engaging online learners: The impact of web-based learning technology on college student engagement". Journal of Educational Technology Development and Exchange (JETDE), 12(1), 9.

[13] Loewen, S., & Isbell, D. R. (2017). "Mobile-assisted language learning: A Duolingo case study". ReCALL, 29(2), 293-311.

[14] Foster, D. (2015). "Cultural exchange and identity development: A study of the impact of Workaway volunteering on young adults". Journal of Youth Studies, 18(5), 605-621.

[15] Kittur, A., Chi, E. H., & Suh, B. (2008). "Crowdsourcing user studies with Mechanical Turk". Proceedings of the SIGCHI conference on human factors in computing systems, 453-456.

Chapter 09: Fostering Community Online: Success Stories from the Virtual World

[1] Reddit. (n.d.). r/AskDocs. Retrieved from https://www.reddit.com/r/AskDocs/

[2] Reddit. (n.d.). r/AskDocs.

[3] 7 Cups. (n.d.). About 7 Cups. Retrieved from https://www.7cups.com/

[4] 7 Cups. (n.d.). About 7 Cups.

[5] LinkedIn. (n.d.). About LinkedIn. Retrieved from https://www.linkedin.com/

[6] LinkedIn. (n.d.). About LinkedIn.

[7] DeviantArt. (n.d.). About DeviantArt. Retrieved from https://www.deviantart.com/

[8] DeviantArt. (n.d.). About DeviantArt.

[9] Khan Academy. (n.d.). About Khan Academy. Retrieved from https://www.khanacademy.org/

[10] Khan Academy. (n.d.). About Khan Academy.

[11] Change.org. (n.d.). About Change.org. Retrieved from https://www.change.org/

[12] Change.org. (n.d.). About Change.org.

[13] Ellison, N. B., Vitak, J., Gray, R., & Lampe, C. (2014). "Cultivating social resources on social network sites: Facebook relationship maintenance behaviors and their role in social capital processes". Journal of Computer-Mediated Communication, 19(4), 855-870.

[14] Boyd, D. M., & Ellison, N. B. (2007). "Social network sites: Definition, history, and scholarship". Journal of Computer-Mediated Communication, 13(1), 210-230.

[15] Kim, A. J. (2000). Community Building on the Web: Secret Strategies for Successful Online Communities. Peachpit Press.

[16] Preece, J., & Maloney-Krichmar, D. (2003). "Online communities: Focusing on sociability and usability". In J. Jacko & A. Sears (Eds.), The Human-Computer Interaction Handbook. Lawrence Erlbaum Associates.

[17] Wellman, B., & Gulia, M. (1999). "Virtual communities as communities: Net surfers don't ride alone". In M. Smith & P. Kollock (Eds.), Communities in Cyberspace. Routledge.

Chapter 10: The Future of Interaction: Innovations Bringing Us Closer

[1] VRChat. (n.d.). Retrieved from https://hello.vrchat.com/

[2] AltspaceVR. (n.d.). Retrieved from https://altvr.com/

[3] Oculus. (n.d.). Oculus Venues. Retrieved from https://www.oculus.com/experiences/quest/section/venue/

[4] Google. (n.d.). Google Meet. Retrieved from https://meet.google.com/

[5] Pokémon Go. (n.d.). Retrieved from https://pokemongolive.com/

[6] Microsoft. (n.d.). Microsoft HoloLens. Retrieved from https://www.microsoft.com/en-us/hololens

[7] Google Translate. (n.d.). Retrieved from https://translate.google.com/

[8] Apple. (n.d.). Siri. Retrieved from https://www.apple.com/siri/

[9] Netflix. (n.d.). How Netflix's Recommendations System Works. Retrieved from https://help.netflix.com/en/node/100639

[10] Woebot. (n.d.). Retrieved from https://woebothealth.com/

[11] IBM. (n.d.). Predictive Analytics. Retrieved from https://www.ibm.com/analytics/predictive-analytics

[12] Amazon. (n.d.). Amazon Echo. Retrieved from https://www.amazon.com/echo/

[13] Fitbit. (n.d.). Retrieved from https://www.fitbit.com/

[14] Smart Cities Council. (n.d.). Retrieved from https://smartcitiescouncil.com/

[15] Nextdoor. (n.d.). Retrieved from https://nextdoor.com/

[16] Steemit. (n.d.). Retrieved from https://steemit.com/

[17] Bitcoin. (n.d.). How Bitcoin Works. Retrieved from https://www.bitcoin.com/get-started/how-bitcoin-works/

Part IV: Rebuilding Our Human Connections

Chapter 11: The Art of Mindful Technology Use: Creating Healthy Digital Habits

[1] Kabat-Zinn, Jon. Wherever You Go, There You Are: Mindfulness Meditation in Everyday Life. Hyperion, 1994.

[2] Turkle, Sherry. Alone Together: Why We Expect More from Technology and Less from Each Other. Basic Books, 2011.

[3] Harris, Dan. 10% Happier: How I Tamed the Voice in My Head, Reduced Stress Without Losing My Edge, and Found Self-Help That Actually Works. Dey Street Books, 2014.

[4] Newport, Cal. Digital Minimalism: Choosing a Focused Life in a Noisy World. Portfolio, 2019.

[5] Price, Catherine. How to Break Up with Your Phone: The 30-Day Plan to Take Back Your Life. Ten Speed Press, 2018.

[6] Alter, Adam. Irresistible: The Rise of Addictive Technology and the Business of Keeping Us Hooked. Penguin Press, 2017.

[7] Goleman, Daniel. Focus: The Hidden Driver of Excellence. Harper, 2013.

[8] McGonigal, Kelly. The Willpower Instinct: How Self-Control Works, Why It Matters, and What You Can Do to Get More of It. Avery, 2011.

[9] Cirillo, Francesco. The Pomodoro Technique: The Life-Changing Time-Management System. Currency, 2018.

[10] Williams, Mark, and Danny Penman. Mindfulness: An Eight-Week Plan for Finding Peace in a Frantic World. Rodale Books, 2011.

[11] Clear, James. Atomic Habits: An Easy & Proven Way to Build Good Habits & Break Bad Ones. Avery, 2018.

[12] Achor, Shawn. The Happiness Advantage: How a Positive Brain Fuels Success in Work and Life. Crown Business, 2010.

[13] Hari, Johann. Lost Connections: Uncovering the Real Causes of Depression – and the Unexpected Solutions. Bloomsbury Publishing, 2018.

[14] Levitin, Daniel J. The Organized Mind: Thinking Straight in the Age of Information Overload. Dutton, 2014.

[15] Brown, Brené. Daring Greatly: How the Courage to Be Vulnerable Transforms the Way We Live, Love, Parent, and Lead. Gotham Books, 2012.

Chapter 12: From Online to Offline: Translating Digital Connections into Real-World Relationships

[1] Turkle, Sherry. Alone Together: Why We Expect More from Technology and Less from Each Other. Basic Books, 2011.

[2] Turkle, Sherry. Reclaiming Conversation: The Power of Talk in a Digital Age. Penguin Press, 2015.

[3] Brown, Brené. Daring Greatly: How the Courage to Be Vulnerable Transforms the Way We Live, Love, Parent, and Lead. Gotham Books, 2012.

[4] Newport, Cal. Digital Minimalism: Choosing a Focused Life in a Noisy World. Portfolio, 2019.

[5] Putnam, Robert D. Bowling Alone: The Collapse and Revival of American Community. Simon & Schuster, 2000.

[6] Harris, Dan. 10% Happier: How I Tamed the Voice in My Head, Reduced Stress Without Losing My Edge, and Found Self-Help That Actually Works. Dey Street Books, 2014.

[7] McGonigal, Kelly. The Willpower Instinct: How Self-Control Works, Why It Matters, and What You Can Do to Get More of It. Avery, 2011.

[8] Cirillo, Francesco. The Pomodoro Technique: The Life-Changing Time-Management System. Currency, 2018.

[9] Price, Catherine. How to Break Up with Your Phone: The 30-Day Plan to Take Back Your Life. Ten Speed Press, 2018.

[10] Kabat-Zinn, Jon. Wherever You Go, There You Are: Mindfulness Meditation in Everyday Life. Hyperion, 1994.

[11] Goleman, Daniel. Emotional Intelligence: Why It Can Matter More Than IQ. Bantam Books, 1995.

[12] Holmes, Leslie. Talk Is Cheap: The Art of Conversation Leadership. Thomas Nelson, 2009.

[13] Clear, James. Atomic Habits: An Easy & Proven Way to Build Good Habits & Break Bad Ones. Avery, 2018.

[14] Achor, Shawn. The Happiness Advantage: How a Positive Brain Fuels Success in Work and Life. Crown Business, 2010.

[15] Patel, Nishta J. The Art of Staying Connected: Strategies for Long-Distance Relationships. Self-published, 2017.

[16] Vlahos, James. Talk to Me: How Voice Computing Will Transform the Way We Live, Work, and Think. Houghton Mifflin Harcourt, 2019.

[17] Alter, Adam. Irresistible: The Rise of Addictive Technology and the Business of Keeping Us Hooked. Penguin Press, 2017.

Chapter 13: Designing for Togetherness: How Developers Can Enhance Human Connection

[1] Turkle, Sherry. Alone Together: Why We Expect More from Technology and Less from Each Other. Basic Books, 2011.

[2] Norman, Donald A. The Design of Everyday Things. Revised and Expanded Edition, Basic Books, 2013.

[3] Lanier, Jaron. Ten Arguments for Deleting Your Social Media Accounts Right Now. Henry Holt and Co., 2018.

[4] Boyd, Danah. It's Complicated: The Social Lives of Networked Teens. Yale University Press, 2014.

[5] Putnam, Robert D. Bowling Alone: The Collapse and Revival of American Community. Simon & Schuster, 2000.

[6] Ellison, Nicole B., et al. "The Benefits of Facebook 'Friends': Social Capital and College Students' Use of Online Social Network Sites." Journal of Computer-Mediated Communication, vol. 12, no. 4, 2007, pp. 1143-1168.

[7] Hu, Yuheng, et al. "Weibo Network, Social Connections and Word of Mouth: Lessons from the Largest Social Media Platform in China." Journal of Marketing Communications, vol. 20, no. 1-2, 2014, pp. 106-123.

[8] Waber, Ben, et al. "Workplace Communication Networks and Productivity." MIT Sloan Management Review, vol. 52, no. 2, 2011, pp. 36-43.

[9] Kowert, Rachel, et al. "Online Gaming, Social Capital, and the Socialization of Place." Games and Culture, vol. 10, no. 4, 2015, pp. 354-373.

[10] Relationships Past and Present." Cyberpsychology, Behavior, and Social Networking, vol. 17, no. 3, 2014, pp. 179-184.

[11] Schroeder, Ralph. Social Interaction in Virtual Environments: Key Issues, Common Themes, and a Framework for Research. Springer, 2014.

[12] Ryan, Richard M., et al. "The Motivational Pull of Video Games: A Self-Determination Theory Approach." Motivation and Emotion, vol. 30, no. 4, 2006, pp. 347-363.

[13] Hampton, Keith N., et al. "Core Networks, Social Isolation, and New Media: How Internet and Mobile Phone Use Is Related to Network Size and Diversity." Information, Communication & Society, vol. 14, no. 1, 2011, pp. 130-155.

[14] Montag, Christian, and Martin Reuter. Internet Addiction: Neuroscientific Approaches and Therapeutical Interventions. Springer, 2017.

[15] Selwyn, Neil. "Digital Inclusion: Can We Ensure That All Citizens Benefit from the Digital Era?" Information, Communication & Society, vol. 7, no. 3, 2004, pp. 364-383.

[16] Acquisti, Alessandro, et al. "Privacy and Human Behavior in the Age of Information." Science, vol. 347, no. 6221, 2015, pp. 509-514.

Chapter 14: Spiritual Solace: Reconnecting with Self and Nature

[1] Pargament, Kenneth I. The Psychology of Religion and Coping: Theory, Research, Practice. Guilford Press, 1997.

[2] Turkle, Sherry. Alone Together: Why We Expect More from Technology and Less from Each Other. Basic Books, 2011.

[3] Kabat-Zinn, Jon. Wherever You Go, There You Are: Mindfulness Meditation in Everyday Life. Hyperion, 1994.

[4] Pennebaker, James W. Writing to Heal: A Guided Journal for Recovering from Trauma & Emotional Upheaval. New Harbinger Publications, 2004.

[5] Newport, Cal. Digital Minimalism: Choosing a Focused Life in a Noisy World. Penguin, 2019.

[6] Nhat Hanh, Thich. Peace Is Every Step: The Path of Mindfulness in Everyday Life. Bantam, 1992.

[7] Louv, Richard. Last Child in the Woods: Saving Our Children from Nature-Deficit Disorder. Algonquin Books, 2005.

8 Kimmerer, Robin Wall. Braiding Sweetgrass: Indigenous Wisdom, Scientific Knowledge, and the Teachings of Plants. Milkweed Editions, 2013.

9 Hanh, Thich Nhat. The Miracle of Mindfulness: An Introduction to the Practice of Meditation. Beacon Press, 1999.

10 Steiner, Rudolf. Nature Spirits: Selected Lectures. Rudolf Steiner Press, 1995.

11 Cottrell, Stella. Mindfulness for Students. Macmillan International Higher Education, 2018.

12 Clear, James. Atomic Habits: An Easy & Proven Way to Build Good Habits & Break Bad Ones. Avery, 2018.

13 Emmons, Robert A., and Michael E. McCullough. "Counting Blessings Versus Burdens: An Experimental Investigation of Gratitude and Subjective Well-Being in Daily Life." Journal of Personality and Social Psychology, vol. 84, no. 2, 2003, pp. 377-389.

14 Siegel, Daniel J. Mind: A Journey to the Heart of Being Human. W.W. Norton & Company, 2016.

15 Putnam, Robert D. Bowling Alone: The Collapse and Revival of American Community. Simon & Schuster, 2000.

16 Baumeister, Roy F., and Mark R. Leary. "The Need to Belong: Desire for Interpersonal Attachments as a Fundamental Human Motivation." Psychological Bulletin, vol. 117, no. 3, 1995, pp. 497-529.

17 Jordan, Catherine, et al. "The Benefits of Volunteering for Older Adults: A Review of Perceived Benefits and Volunteering." The Gerontologist, vol. 38, no. 4, 1998, pp. 531-539.

NOTES:

BIBLIOGRAPGHY

Part I: Understanding Our Loneliness

Chapter 01: The Evolution of Communication: From Face-to-Face to Digital Interfaces

1. Tomasello, Michael. *The Origins of Human Communication*. MIT Press, 2008.
2. Falk, Dean. *Prelinguistic Evolution in Early Hominins: Whence Motherese?* MIT Press, 2009.
3. Harari, Yuval Noah. *Sapiens: A Brief History of Humankind*. Harper, 2015.
4. Martin, Henri-Jean. *The History and Power of Writing*. University of Chicago Press, 1994.
5. Schmandt-Besserat, Denise. *How Writing Came About*. University of Texas Press, 1996.
6. Eisenstein, Elizabeth L. *The Printing Revolution in Early Modern Europe*. Cambridge University Press, 1983.
7. Christie, Alix. *Gutenberg's Apprentice*. Harper, 2014.
8. Johns, Adrian. *The Nature of the Book: Print and Knowledge in the Making*. University of Chicago Press, 1998.
9. Standage, Tom. *The Victorian Internet: The Remarkable Story of the Telegraph and the Nineteenth Century's On-line Pioneers*. Walker & Co., 1998.
10. Seidman, David. *Samuel Morse and the Telegraph*. The Rosen Publishing Group, 2003.
11. Gleick, James. *The Information: A History, a Theory, a Flood*. Pantheon Books, 2011.
12. Shulman, Seth. *The Telephone Gambit: Chasing Alexander Graham Bell's Secret*. W.W. Norton & Company, 2008.
13. Casson, Herbert N. *A History of the Telephone*. Ayer Co., 1983.
14. Jonnes, Jill. *Empires of Light: Edison, Tesla, Westinghouse, and the Race to Electrify the World*. Random House, 2004.

15. Carr, Nicholas. *The Shallows: What the Internet Is Doing to Our Brains*. W.W. Norton & Company, 2010.

16. Turkle, Sherry. *Alone Together: Why We Expect More from Technology and Less from Each Other*. Basic Books, 2011.

17. Castells, Manuel. *The Internet Galaxy: Reflections on the Internet, Business, and Society*. Oxford University Press, 2001.

18. Twenge, Jean M. *iGen: Why Today's Super-Connected Kids Are Growing Up Less Rebellious, More Tolerant, Less Happy*. Atria Books, 2017.

19. Newport, Cal. *Digital Minimalism: Choosing a Focused Life in a Noisy World*. Portfolio, 2019.

20. Alter, Adam. *Irresistible: The Rise of Addictive Technology and the Business of Keeping Us Hooked*. Penguin Press, 2017.

21. Rheingold, Howard. *The Virtual Community: Homesteading on the Electronic Frontier*. MIT Press, 1993.

22. Gordon, Eric, and Adriana de Souza e Silva. *Net Locality: Why Location Matters in a Networked World*. Wiley-Blackwell, 2011.

23. Bailenson, Jeremy. *Experience on Demand: What Virtual Reality Is, How It Works, and What It Can Do*. W.W. Norton & Company, 2018.

Chapter 02: The Illusion of Connectedness: Social Media's False Promises

1. Turkle, S. (2011). Alone Together: Why We Expect More from Technology and Less from Each Other. Basic Books.

2. Derks, D., Fischer, A. H., & Bos, A. E. (2008). "The Role of Emotion in Computer-Mediated Communication: A Review". Computers in Human Behavior, 24(3), 766-785.

3. Goffman, E. (1959). The Presentation of Self in Everyday Life. Anchor Books.

4. Kross, E., Verduyn, P., Demiralp, E., Park, J., Lee, D. S., Lin, N., ... & Ybarra, O. (2013). "Facebook Use Predicts Declines in Subjective Well-Being in Young Adults". PLOS One, 8(8), e69841.

5. Przybylski, A. K., Murayama, K., DeHaan, C. R., & Gladwell, V. (2013). "Motivational, Emotional, and Behavioral Correlates of Fear of Missing Out". Computers in Human Behavior, 29(4), 1841-1848.

6. Alter, A. (2017). Irresistible: The Rise of Addictive Technology and the Business of Keeping Us Hooked. Penguin Press.

7. Schwartz, B. (2004). The Paradox of Choice: Why More Is Less. HarperCollins.

8. Lu, H., & Sundar, S. S. (2012). "An Examination of the Effects of Technological Attributes on Adolescents' Unhealthy Information Disclosure Behavior on Social Network Sites". Cyberpsychology, Behavior, and Social Networking, 15(2), 105-110.

9. Pariser, E. (2011). The Filter Bubble: How the New Personalized Web Is Changing What We Read and How We Think. Penguin Press.

10. Boyd, D. (2014). It's Complicated: The Social Lives of Networked Teens. Yale University Press.

11. Aiken, M. (2016). The Cyber Effect: A Pioneering Cyberpsychologist Explains How Human Behavior Changes Online. Spiegel & Grau.

12. Przybylski, A. K., Murayama, K., DeHaan, C. R., & Gladwell, V. (2013). "Motivational, Emotional, and Behavioral Correlates of Fear of Missing Out". Computers in Human Behavior, 29(4), 1841-1848.

13. Alter, A. (2017). Irresistible: The Rise of Addictive Technology and the Business of Keeping Us Hooked. Penguin Press.

14. Lu, H., & Sundar, S. S. (2012). "An Examination of the Effects of Technological Attributes on Adolescents' Unhealthy Information Disclosure Behavior on Social Network Sites". Cyberpsychology, Behavior, and Social Networking, 15(2), 105-110.

15. Pariser, E. (2011). The Filter Bubble: How the New Personalized Web Is Changing What We Read and How We Think. Penguin Press.

16. Boyd, D. (2014). It's Complicated: The Social Lives of Networked Teens. Yale University Press.

17. Aiken, M. (2016). The Cyber Effect: A Pioneering Cyberpsychologist Explains How Human Behavior Changes Online. Spiegel & Grau.

18. Johnson, R. (2020). "How Zoom Became the Hero of the Pandemic". The New York Times. Retrieved from https://www.nytimes.com/2020/04/06/technology/zoom-technology-coronavirus.html.

19. Smith, A. (2020). "How the Pandemic Is Changing Digital Communication". Harvard Business Review. Retrieved from https://hbr.org/2020/03/how-the-pandemic-is-changing-digital-communication

Chapter 03: Connecting Across Landscapes: Technology's Impact on Social Bonds in Urban, Suburban, and Rural Areas

1. Klinenberg, E. (2012). Going Solo: The Extraordinary Rise and Surprising Appeal of Living Alone. Penguin Books.
2. Hampton, K. N., & Wellman, B. (2003). "Neighboring in Netville: How the Internet Supports Community and Social Capital in a Wired Suburb". City & Community, 2(4), 277-311.
3. Putnam, R. D. (2000). Bowling Alone: The Collapse and Revival of American Community. Simon & Schuster.
4. Turkle, S. (2011). Alone Together: Why We Expect More from Technology and Less from Each Other. Basic Books.
5. Fischer, C. S. (1992). America Calling: A Social History of the Telephone to 1940. University of California Press.
6. Smith, A. (2018). "How Americans Encounter, Recall and Act Upon Digital News". Pew Research Center. Retrieved from https://www.pewresearch.org/internet/2018/02/09/how-americans-encounter-recall-and-act-upon-digital-news/.
7. Ellison, N. B., & Boyd, D. (2013). "Sociality through Social Network Sites". In Dutton, W. H. (Ed.), The Oxford Handbook of Internet Studies. Oxford University Press.
8. Alter, A. (2017). Irresistible: The Rise of Addictive Technology and the Business of Keeping Us Hooked. Penguin Press.
9. Lu, H., & Sundar, S. S. (2012). "An Examination of the Effects of Technological Attributes on Adolescents' Unhealthy Information Disclosure Behavior on Social Network Sites". Cyberpsychology, Behavior, and Social Networking, 15(2), 105-110.
10. Granovetter, M. (1983). "The Strength of Weak Ties: A Network Theory Revisited". Sociological Theory, 1, 201-233.
11. Pariser, E. (2011). The Filter Bubble: How the New Personalized Web Is Changing What We Read and How We Think. Penguin Press.
12. Anderson, M., & Perrin, A. (2018). "Nearly One-in-Five Teens Can't Always Finish Their Homework Because of the Digital Divide". Pew Research Center. Retrieved from https://www.pewresearch.org/fact-tank/2018/10/26/nearly-one-in-five-teens-cant-always-finish-their-homework-because-of-the-digital-divide/.

13. Aiken, M. (2016). The Cyber Effect: A Pioneering Cyberpsychologist Explains How Human Behavior Changes Online. Spiegel & Grau.

Chapter 04: "The Psychology of Loneliness: Recognizing the Inner Signs

1. Hawkley, L. C., & Cacioppo, J. T. (2010). "Loneliness Matters: A Theoretical and Empirical Review of Consequences and Mechanisms". Annals of Behavioral Medicine, 40(2), 218-227.

2. Lim, M. H., Rodebaugh, T. L., Zyphur, M. J., & Gleeson, J. F. (2016). "Loneliness Over Time: The Crucial Role of Social Anxiety". Journal of Abnormal Psychology, 125(5), 620-630.

3. Leary, M. R. (1990). "Responses to Social Exclusion: Social Anxiety, Jealousy, Loneliness, Depression, and Low Self-Esteem". Journal of Social and Clinical Psychology, 9(2), 221-229.

4. Mikulincer, M., & Shaver, P. R. (2007). Attachment in Adulthood: Structure, Dynamics, and Change. Guilford Press.

5. Victor, C. R., Scambler, S. J., Bowling, A., & Bond, J. (2005). "The Prevalence of, and Risk Factors for, Loneliness in Later Life: A Survey of Older People in Great Britain". Ageing and Society, 25(6), 357-375.

6. Cacioppo, J. T., & Patrick, W. (2008). Loneliness: Human Nature and the Need for Social Connection. W. W. Norton & Company.

7. Heinrich, L. M., & Gullone, E. (2006). "The Clinical Significance of Loneliness: A Literature Review". Clinical Psychology Review, 26(6), 695-718.

8. Nolen-Hoeksema, S., Wisco, B. E., & Lyubomirsky, S. (2008). "Rethinking Rumination". Perspectives on Psychological Science, 3(5), 400-424.

9. Qualter, P., Vanhalst, J., Harris, R., Van Roekel, E., Lodder, G., Bangee, M., & Verhagen, M. (2015). "Loneliness Across the Life Span". Perspectives on Psychological Science, 10(2), 250-264.

10. Hawkley, L. C., Thisted, R. A., & Cacioppo, J. T. (2009). "Loneliness Predicts Reduced Physical Activity: Cross-Sectional & Longitudinal Analyses". Health Psychology, 28(3), 354-363.

11. Cacioppo, J. T., Hughes, M. E., Waite, L. J., Hawkley, L. C., & Thisted, R. A. (2006). "Loneliness as a Specific Risk Factor for Depressive Symptoms: Cross-Sectional and Longitudinal Analyses". Psychology and Aging, 21(1), 140-151.

12. Beutel, M. E., Klein, E. M., Brähler, E., Reiner, I., Jünger, C., Michal, M., ... & Tibubos, A. N. (2017). "Loneliness in the General Population: Prevalence, Determinants and Relations to Mental Health". BMC Psychiatry, 17(1), 1-7.

13. Cacioppo, J. T., & Hawkley, L. C. (2009). "Perceived Social Isolation and Cognition". Trends in Cognitive Sciences, 13(10), 447-454.

14. Holt-Lunstad, J., Smith, T. B., & Layton, J. B. (2010). "Social Relationships and Mortality Risk: A Meta-analytic Review". PLOS Medicine, 7(7), e1000316.

15. Masi, C. M., Chen, H. Y., Hawkley, L. C., & Cacioppo, J. T. (2011). "A Meta-Analysis of Interventions to Reduce Loneliness". Personality and Social Psychology Review, 15(3), 219-266.

16. Neff, K. D. (2003). "Self-Compassion: An Alternative Conceptualization of a Healthy Attitude Toward Oneself". Self and Identity, 2(2), 85-101.

17. Steger, M. F., Oishi, S., & Kashdan, T. B. (2009). "Meaning in Life Across the Life Span: Levels and Correlates of Meaning in Life from Emerging Adulthood to Older Adulthood". The Journal of Positive Psychology, 4(1), 43-52.

18. Nowland, R., Necka, E. A., & Cacioppo, J. T. (2018). "Loneliness and Social Internet Use: Pathways to Reconnection in a Digital World?". Perspectives on Psychological Science, 13(1), 70-87.

Part II: The Irony of Technology-Induced Isolation

Chapter 05: When Phones Replace Humans: The Impact of Screen Time on Personal Relationships

1. Smith, A. (2018). "The smartphone is the most transformative invention of the 21st century". Pew Research Center. Retrieved from https://www.pewresearch.org.

2. Roberts, J. A., & David, M. E. (2016). "My life has become a major distraction from my cell phone: Partner phubbing and relationship satisfaction among romantic partners". Computers in Human Behavior, 54, 134-141.

3. Przybylski, A. K., & Weinstein, N. (2013). "Can you connect with me now? How the presence of mobile communication technology influences face-to-face conversation quality". Journal of Social and Personal Relationships, 30(3), 325-335.

4. Misra, S., Cheng, L., Genevie, J., & Yuan, M. (2016). "The iPhone effect: The quality of in-person social interactions in the presence of mobile devices". Environment and Behavior, 48(2), 275-298.

5. Konrath, S. H., O'Brien, E. H., & Hsing, C. (2011). "Changes in dispositional empathy in American college students over time: A meta-analysis". Personality and Social Psychology Review, 15(2), 180-198.

6. Twenge, J. M., & Campbell, W. K. (2018). "Associations between screen time and lower psychological well-being among children and adolescents: Evidence from a population-based study". Preventive Medicine Reports, 12, 271-283.

7. McDaniel, B. T., & Coyne, S. M. (2016). ""Technoference": The interference of technology in couple relationships and implications for women's personal and relational well-being". Psychology of Popular Media Culture, 5(1), 85-98.

8. Kabat-Zinn, J. (1994). Wherever you go, there you are: Mindfulness meditation in everyday life. Hyperion.

9. Turkle, S. (2017). Reclaiming conversation: The power of talk in a digital age. Penguin Books.

Chapter 06: The End of Privacy: How Constant Connectivity Can Create Distance

1. Papacharissi, Z. (2010). A Private Sphere: Democracy in a Digital Age. Polity Press.

2. Marwick, A. E., & boyd, d. (2014). "Networked privacy: How teenagers negotiate context in social media". New Media & Society, 16(7), 1051-1067.

3. Turkle, S. (2011). Alone Together: Why We Expect More from Technology and Less from Each Other. Basic Books.

4. Tufekci, Z. (2017). Twitter and Tear Gas: The Power and Fragility of Networked Protest. Yale University Press.

5. Fuchs, C. (2011). "New Media, Web 2.0 and Surveillance". Sociological Compass, 5(2), 134-147.

6. Przybylski, A. K., Murayama, K., DeHaan, C. R., & Gladwell, V. (2013). "Motivational, emotional, and behavioral correlates of fear of missing out". Computers in Human Behavior, 29(4), 1841-1848.

7. Chou, H. T. G., & Edge, N. (2012). "They are happier and having better lives than I am: The impact of using Facebook on perceptions of others' lives". Cyberpsychology, Behavior, and Social Networking, 15(2), 117-121.

8. Boyd, d. (2014). It's Complicated: The Social Lives of Networked Teens. Yale University Press.

9. Suttie, J. (2019). "How to Cultivate Meaningful Connections Offline". Greater Good Magazine. Retrieved from https://greatergood.berkeley.edu.

10. Roberts, J. A., & David, M. E. (2020). "The Social Media See-Saw: Positive and Negative Influences on Adolescents' Affective Well-Being". Teens and Technology.

11. Neff, K. D. (2011). Self-Compassion: The Proven Power of Being Kind to Yourself. William Morrow.

12. Harris, F. M., & Jones, S. R. (2019). "Understanding the Impact of Digital Media on Mental Health and Well-Being". Journal of Adolescent Health, 65(6), 700-703.

Chapter 07: Echo Chambers and Filter Bubbles: Losing the Human Touch

1. Sunstein, C. R. (2001). Echo Chambers: Bush v. Gore, Impeachment, and Beyond. Princeton University Press.

2. Pariser, E. (2011). The Filter Bubble: How the New Personalized Web Is Changing What We Read and How We Think. Penguin Press.

3. Nickerson, R. S. (1998). "Confirmation Bias: A Ubiquitous Phenomenon in Many Guises". Review of General Psychology, 2(2), 175-220.

4. Garrett, R. K. (2009). "Echo chambers online? Politically motivated selective exposure among Internet news users". Journal of Computer-Mediated Communication, 14(2), 265-285.

5. Sunstein, C. R. (2018). #Republic: Divided Democracy in the Age of Social Media. Princeton University Press.

6. Turkle, S. (2011). Alone Together: Why We Expect More from Technology and Less from Each Other. Basic Books.

7. Bail, C. A., Argyle, L. P., Brown, T. W., Bumpus, J. P., Chen, H., Hunzaker, M. B. F., ... & Volfovsky, A. (2018). "Exposure to opposing views on social media can increase political polarization". Proceedings of the National Academy of Sciences, 115(37), 9216-9221.

8. Iyengar, S., & Westwood, S. J. (2015). "Fear and loathing across party lines: New evidence on group polarization". American Journal of Political Science, 59(3), 690-707.

9. Guess, A., Nyhan, B., & Reifler, J. (2018). "Selective exposure to misinformation: Evidence from the consumption of fake news during the 2016 US presidential campaign". European Research Council.

10. Coleman, S. (2013). How Voters Feel. Cambridge University Press.

11. Bakshy, E., Messing, S., & Adamic, L. A. (2015). "Exposure to ideologically diverse news and opinion on Facebook". Science, 348(6239), 1130-1132.

12. Kahneman, D. (2011). Thinking, Fast and Slow. Farrar, Straus and Giroux.

13. Dunbar, R. I. M. (2016). "Do online social media cut through the constraints that limit the size of offline social networks?". Royal Society Open Science, 3(1), 150292.

14. Davis, M. H. (1996). Empathy: A Social Psychological Approach. Westview Press.

15. Putnam, R. D. (2000). Bowling Alone: The Collapse and Revival of American Community. Simon & Schuster.

16. Brown, B. (2012). Daring Greatly: How the Courage to Be Vulnerable Transforms the Way We Live, Love, Parent, and Lead. Gotham Books.

Part III: Technology as a Bridge, Not a Barrier

Chapter 08: Digital Tools for Real Connection: The Positive Side of Tech

1. Ellison, N. B., Vitak, J., Gray, R., & Lampe, C. (2014). "Cultivating social resources on social network sites: Facebook relationship maintenance behaviors and their role in social capital processes". Journal of Computer-Mediated Communication, 19(4), 855-870.

2. Church, K., & de Oliveira, R. (2013). "What's up with WhatsApp? Comparing mobile instant messaging behaviors with traditional SMS". Proceedings of the 15th international conference on Human-computer interaction with mobile devices and services, 352-361.

3. Zhang, R. (2016). "The stress-buffering effect of self-disclosure on Facebook: An examination of stressful life events, social support, and mental health among college students". Computers in Human Behavior, 75, 527-537.

4. Gilbert, E., & Karahalios, K. (2009). "Predicting tie strength with social media". Proceedings of the SIGCHI Conference on Human Factors in Computing Systems, 211-220.

5. Hartzog, P. (2007). "The commons as an emerging mode of social organization in the information age". Information, Communication & Society, 10(6), 766-785.

6. Finkel, E. J., Eastwick, P. W., Karney, B. R., Reis, H. T., & Sprecher, S. (2012). "Online dating: A critical analysis from the perspective of psychological science". Psychological Science in the Public Interest, 13(1), 3-66.

7. Firth, J., Torous, J., Nicholas, J., Carney, R., Pratap, A., Rosenbaum, S., & Sarris, J. (2017). "The efficacy of smartphone-based mental health interventions for depressive symptoms: a meta-analysis of randomized controlled trials". World Psychiatry, 16(3), 287-298.

8. Richards, D., & Viganó, N. (2013). "Online counseling: A narrative and critical review of the literature". Journal of Clinical Psychology, 69(9), 994-1011.

9. DeAndrea, D. C., & Walther, J. B. (2011). "Attributions for inconsistencies between online and offline self-presentations". Communication Research, 38(6), 805-825.

10. Boyd, D. M., & Ellison, N. B. (2007). "Social network sites: Definition, history, and scholarship". Journal of Computer-Mediated Communication, 13(1), 210-230.

11. Mazman, S. G., & Usluel, Y. K. (2010). "Modeling educational usage of Facebook". Computers & Education, 55(2), 444-453.

12. Yu, J., & Liu, Y. (2020). "Engaging online learners: The impact of web-based learning technology on college student engagement". Journal of Educational Technology Development and Exchange (JETDE), 12(1), 9.

13. Loewen, S., & Isbell, D. R. (2017). "Mobile-assisted language learning: A Duolingo case study". ReCALL, 29(2), 293-311.

14. Foster, D. (2015). "Cultural exchange and identity development: A study of the impact of Workaway volunteering on young adults". Journal of Youth Studies, 18(5), 605-621.

15. Kittur, A., Chi, E. H., & Suh, B. (2008). "Crowdsourcing user studies with Mechanical Turk". Proceedings of the SIGCHI conference on human factors in computing systems, 453-456.

Chapter 09: Fostering Community Online: Success Stories from the Virtual World

1. Reddit. (n.d.). r/AskDocs. Retrieved from https://www.reddit.com/r/AskDocs/

2. 7 Cups. (n.d.). About 7 Cups. Retrieved from https://www.7cups.com/

3. LinkedIn. (n.d.). About LinkedIn. Retrieved from https://www.linkedin.com/

4. DeviantArt. (n.d.). About DeviantArt. Retrieved from https://www.deviantart.com/

5. Khan Academy. (n.d.). About Khan Academy. Retrieved from https://www.khanacademy.org/

6. Change.org. (n.d.). About Change.org. Retrieved from https://www.change.org/

7. Ellison, N. B., Vitak, J., Gray, R., & Lampe, C. (2014). "Cultivating social resources on social network sites: Facebook relationship maintenance behaviors and their role in social capital processes". Journal of Computer-Mediated Communication, 19(4), 855-870.

8. Boyd, D. M., & Ellison, N. B. (2007). "Social network sites: Definition, history, and scholarship". Journal of Computer-Mediated Communication, 13(1), 210-230.

9. Kim, A. J. (2000). Community Building on the Web: Secret Strategies for Successful Online Communities. Peachpit Press.

10. Preece, J., & Maloney-Krichmar, D. (2003). "Online communities: Focusing on sociability and usability". In J. Jacko & A. Sears (Eds.), The Human-Computer Interaction Handbook. Lawrence Erlbaum Associates.

11. Wellman, B., & Gulia, M. (1999). "Virtual communities as communities: Net surfers don't ride alone". In M. Smith & P. Kollock (Eds.), Communities in Cyberspace. Routledge.

Chapter 10: The Future of Interaction: Innovations Bringing Us Closer

1. VRChat. (n.d.). Retrieved from https://hello.vrchat.com/

2. AltspaceVR. (n.d.). Retrieved from https://altvr.com/

3. Oculus. (n.d.). Oculus Venues. Retrieved from https://www.oculus.com/experiences/quest/section/venue/

4. Google. (n.d.). Google Meet. Retrieved from https://meet.google.com/

5. Pokémon Go. (n.d.). Retrieved from https://pokemongolive.com/

6. Microsoft. (n.d.). Microsoft HoloLens. Retrieved from https://www.microsoft.com/en-us/hololens

7. Google Translate. (n.d.). Retrieved from https://translate.google.com/

8. Apple. (n.d.). Siri. Retrieved from https://www.apple.com/siri/

9. Netflix. (n.d.). How Netflix's Recommendations System Works. Retrieved from https://help.netflix.com/en/node/100639

10. Woebot. (n.d.). Retrieved from https://woebothealth.com/

11. IBM. (n.d.). Predictive Analytics. Retrieved from https://www.ibm.com/analytics/predictive-analytics

12. Amazon. (n.d.). Amazon Echo. Retrieved from https://www.amazon.com/echo/

13. Fitbit. (n.d.). Retrieved from https://www.fitbit.com/

14. Smart Cities Council. (n.d.). Retrieved from https://smartcitiescouncil.com/

15. Nextdoor. (n.d.). Retrieved from https://nextdoor.com/

16. Steemit. (n.d.). Retrieved from https://steemit.com/

17. Bitcoin. (n.d.). How Bitcoin Works. Retrieved from https://www.bitcoin.com/get-started/how-bitcoin-works/

Part IV: Rebuilding Our Human Connections

Chapter 11: The Art of Mindful Technology Use: Creating Healthy Digital Habits

1. Achor, Shawn. The Happiness Advantage: How a Positive Brain Fuels Success in Work and Life. Crown Business, 2010.

2. Alter, Adam. Irresistible: The Rise of Addictive Technology and the Business of Keeping Us Hooked. Penguin Press, 2017.

3. Brown, Brené. Daring Greatly: How the Courage to Be Vulnerable Transforms the Way We Live, Love, Parent, and Lead. Gotham Books, 2012.

4. Cirillo, Francesco. The Pomodoro Technique: The Life-Changing Time-Management System. Currency, 2018.

5. Clear, James. Atomic Habits: An Easy & Proven Way to Build Good Habits & Break Bad Ones. Avery, 2018.

6. Goleman, Daniel. Focus: The Hidden Driver of Excellence. Harper, 2013.

7. Hari, Johann. Lost Connections: Uncovering the Real Causes of Depression – and the Unexpected Solutions. Bloomsbury Publishing, 2018.

8. Harris, Dan. 10% Happier: How I Tamed the Voice in My Head, Reduced Stress Without Losing My Edge, and Found Self-Help That Actually Works. Dey Street Books, 2014.

9. Kabat-Zinn, Jon. Wherever You Go, There You Are: Mindfulness Meditation in Everyday Life. Hyperion, 1994.

10. Levitin, Daniel J. The Organized Mind: Thinking Straight in the Age of Information Overload. Dutton, 2014.

11. McGonigal, Kelly. The Willpower Instinct: How Self-Control Works, Why It Matters, and What You Can Do to Get More of It. Avery, 2011.

12. Newport, Cal. Digital Minimalism: Choosing a Focused Life in a Noisy World. Portfolio, 2019.

13. Price, Catherine. How to Break Up with Your Phone: The 30-Day Plan to Take Back Your Life. Ten Speed Press, 2018.

Turkle, Sherry. Alone Together: Why We Expect More from Technology and Less from Each Other. Basic Books, 2011.

Williams, Mark, and Danny Penman. Mindfulness: An Eight-Week Plan for Finding Peace in a Frantic World. Rodale Books, 2011.

Chapter 12: From Online to Offline: Translating Digital Connections into Real-World Relationships

1. Achor, Shawn. The Happiness Advantage: How a Positive Brain Fuels Success in Work and Life. Crown Business, 2010.

2. Alter, Adam. Irresistible: The Rise of Addictive Technology and the Business of Keeping Us Hooked. Penguin Press, 2017.

3. Brown, Brené. Daring Greatly: How the Courage to Be Vulnerable Transforms the Way We Live, Love, Parent, and Lead. Gotham Books, 2012.

4. Cirillo, Francesco. The Pomodoro Technique: The Life-Changing Time-Management System. Currency, 2018.

5. Clear, James. Atomic Habits: An Easy & Proven Way to Build Good Habits & Break Bad Ones. Avery, 2018.

6. Goleman, Daniel. Emotional Intelligence: Why It Can Matter More Than IQ. Bantam Books, 1995.

7. Harris, Dan. 10% Happier: How I Tamed the Voice in My Head, Reduced Stress Without Losing My Edge, and Found Self-Help That Actually Works. Dey Street Books, 2014.

8. Holmes, Leslie. Talk Is Cheap: The Art of Conversation Leadership. Thomas Nelson, 2009.

9. Kabat-Zinn, Jon. Wherever You Go, There You Are: Mindfulness Meditation in Everyday Life. Hyperion, 1994.

10. McGonigal, Kelly. The Willpower Instinct: How Self-Control Works, Why It Matters, and What You Can Do to Get More of It. Avery, 2011.

11. Newport, Cal. Digital Minimalism: Choosing a Focused Life in a Noisy World. Portfolio, 2019.

12. Patel, Nishta J. The Art of Staying Connected: Strategies for Long-Distance Relationships. Self-published, 2017.

13. Price, Catherine. How to Break Up with Your Phone: The 30-Day Plan to Take Back Your Life. Ten Speed Press, 2018.

14. Putnam, Robert D. Bowling Alone: The Collapse and Revival of American Community. Simon & Schuster, 2000.

15. Turkle, Sherry. Alone Together: Why We Expect More from Technology and Less from Each Other. Basic Books, 2011.

16. Turkle, Sherry. Reclaiming Conversation: The Power of Talk in a Digital Age. Penguin Press, 2015.

17. Vlahos, James. Talk to Me: How Voice Computing Will Transform the Way We Live, Work, and Think. Houghton Mifflin Harcourt, 2019.

Chapter 13: Designing for Togetherness: How Developers Can Enhance Human Connection

1. Alter, Adam. Irresistible: The Rise of Addictive Technology and the Business of Keeping Us Hooked. Penguin Press, 2017.

2. Anderson, Monica, and Madhumitha Kumar. "Digital Divide Persists Even as Lower-Income Americans Make Gains in Tech Adoption." Pew Research Center, 2019.

3. Brown, Brené. Daring Greatly: How the Courage to Be Vulnerable Transforms the Way We Live, Love, Parent, and Lead. Gotham Books, 2012. Finkel, Eli J., et al. "The Suffocation of Marriage: Climbing Mount Maslow Without Enough Oxygen." Psychological Inquiry, vol. 25, no. 1, 2014, pp. 1-41.

4. Frier, Sarah. No Filter: The Inside Story of Instagram. Simon & Schuster, 2020.

5. Goleman, Daniel. Emotional Intelligence: Why It Can Matter More Than IQ. Bantam Books, 1995.

6. Kabat-Zinn, Jon. Full Catastrophe Living: Using the Wisdom of Your Body and Mind to Face Stress, Pain, and Illness. Delta, 1990.

7. Lee, Min Kyung, et al. "The Impact of Neighborhood Networks on Civic Engagement." Proceedings of the 2019 CHI Conference on Human Factors in Computing Systems, 2019.

8. McNamee, Roger. Zucked: Waking Up to the Facebook Catastrophe. Penguin Press, 2019.

9. Niemeyer, Greg. "Video Conferencing and Empathy." Journal of Visual Culture, vol. 19, no. 2, 2020, pp. 207-222.

10. Norman, Donald A. The Design of Everyday Things: Revised and Expanded Edition. Basic Books, 2013.

11. Schroeder, Ralph. Social Interaction in Virtual Environments: Key Issues, Common Themes, and a Framework for Research. Springer-Verlag, 2011.

12. Steinkuehler, Constance, and Dmitri Williams. "Where Everybody Knows Your (Screen) Name: Online Games as 'Third Places'." Journal of Computer-Mediated Communication, vol. 11, no. 4, 2006, pp. 885-909.

13. Turkle, Sherry. Reclaiming Conversation: The Power of Talk in a Digital Age. Penguin Press, 2015.

14. Wenger, Etienne. Communities of Practice: Learning, Meaning, and Identity. Cambridge University Press, 1998.

Chapter 14: Spiritual Solace: Reconnecting with Self and Nature

1. Adams, Kathleen. Journal to the Self: Twenty-Two Paths to Personal Growth. Warner Books, 1990.

2. Csikszentmihalyi, Mihaly. Flow: The Psychology of Optimal Experience. Harper & Row, 1990.

3. Emmons, Robert A. Thanks!: How Practicing Gratitude Can Make You Happier. Houghton Mifflin Harcourt, 2007.

4. Emmons, Robert A., and Michael E. McCullough. "Counting Blessings versus Burdens: An Experimental Investigation of Gratitude and Subjective Well-Being in Daily Life." Journal of Personality and Social Psychology, vol. 84, no. 2, 2003, pp. 377-389.

5. Harris, Dan. 10% Happier: How I Tamed the Voice in My Head, Reduced Stress Without Losing My Edge, and Found Self-Help That Actually Works. Dey Street Books, 2014.

6. Kabat-Zinn, Jon. Wherever You Go, There You Are: Mindfulness Meditation in Everyday Life. Hyperion, 1994.

7. Kaplan, Rachel, and Stephen Kaplan. The Experience of Nature: A Psychological Perspective. Cambridge University Press, 1989.

8. Louv, Richard. Last Child in the Woods: Saving Our Children from Nature-Deficit Disorder. Algonquin Books, 2005.
McGonigal, Kelly. The Willpower Instinct: How Self-Control Works, Why It Matters, and What You Can Do to Get More of It. Avery, 2011.

9. Nestor, James. Breath: The New Science of a Lost Art. Riverhead Books, 2020.

10. Palmer, Parker J. Let Your Life Speak: Listening for the Voice of Vocation. Jossey-Bass, 2000.

11. Plotkin, Bill. Soulcraft: Crossing into the Mysteries of Nature and Psyche. New World Library, 2003.

12. Price, Catherine. How to Break Up with Your Phone: The 30-Day Plan to Take Back Your Life. Ten Speed Press, 2018.

13. Putnam, Robert D. Bowling Alone: The Collapse and Revival of American Community. Simon & Schuster, 2000.

14. Turkle, Sherry. Alone Together: Why We Expect More from Technology and Less from Each Other. Basic Books, 2011.

15. White, Randy. "The Therapeutic Benefits of Gardening." Journal of Therapeutic Horticulture, vol. 27, no. 1, 2017, pp. 22-30.

NOTES:

www.ingramcontent.com/pod-product-compliance
Lightning Source LLC
Chambersburg PA
CBHW070052080526
44586CB00013B/1019